QU(E)ERYING EVANGELISM

The Center for Lesbian and Gay Studies in Religion and Ministry

Pacific School of Religion
1798 Scenic Avenue
Berkeley, California 94709
Phone: (800) 999-0528
Fax: (510) 849-8212
www.clgs.org

QU(E)ERYING EVANGELISM

EVANGELISM

GROWING A COMMUNITY

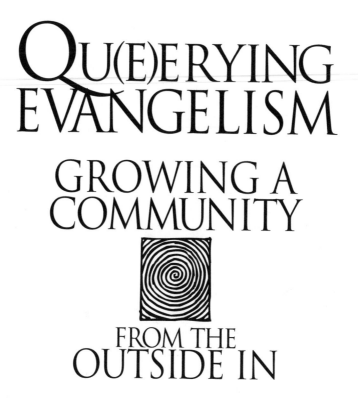

FROM THE OUTSIDE IN

Cheri DiNovo

THE
PILGRIM
PRESS
Cleveland

Euangelos: from the Greek: angel, messenger

To all the angels at
Emmanuel Howard Park United Church
and Toby Dancer

The Pilgrim Press
700 Prospect Avenue
Cleveland, Ohio 44115-1100
thepilgrimpress.com

Scripture quotations are from the New Revised Standard Version Bible, copy-
right © 1993 by the Division of Christian Education of the National Council
of the Churches of Christ in the U.S.A. All rights reserved.

Printed in the United States of America on acid-free paper

09 08 07 06 05   5 4 3 2 1

Library of Congress Cataloging-in-Publication Data

DiNovo, Cheri, 1959-
      Qu(e)erying evangelism : growing a community from the outside in /
Cheri DiNovo.
          p.   cm.
      Includes bibliographical references (p.   )
      ISBN 0-8298-1687-9 (pbk. : alk. paper)
      1. Church growth. 2. Church work with gays. 3. City churches.
I. Title: Queerying evangelism. II. Querying evangelism.   III. Title.
BV652.25.D56 2005
259′.086′64 – dc22

2005049299

Contents

Foreword

Gayatri Spivak, an important contemporary postcolonial theorist, entitled her famous 1988 essay, "Can the Subaltern Speak?"[1] in order to ask whether the Indian people who lived under the colonial power of the West could ever truly speak in their own voices. In the end, she decides they could not because their representation in society was always crafted not by themselves, but by the dominant voices of the colonizers' discourse, in which the colonized masses existed primarily as abstractions to be pointed to, not as real people with their own lives and views. They were the objects of social discourse, never its subjects. While the differences between the formerly colonized people of India and those who today identify as part of the lesbian, gay, transgender, bisexual, or queer communities is vast, the situation of being the objectified, silenced "Other" within the discourses of the dominant culture is remarkably similar.

Over the past century particularly, as debates over the moral and civil status of sexual minority groups have raged in churches, halls of government, courts, professional associations, and city streets, the loudest and often the only voices heard were those of the dominant heterosexual majority. Whether those voices were raised in denigration or, more rarely, in support, bisexuals, lesbians, gay men, and transgender people themselves were often visible only as silent abstractions within the violent logic of homophobia and heterosexism. They were allowed little or no public voice; whatever knowledge they possessed about their own situations was deemed inadequate, naive, biased, or simply irrelevant to the debate about them. The elite experts of the dominant heterosexual group, the doctors, lawyers, politicians, clergy, and scholars, established themselves as the only reliable sources of knowledge about those "others" whom their "expert witness" often condemned to silence — or worse.

Fortunately, within the last fifteen years much of this enforced public silence has been shaken off by the concerted action of sexual

---

1. Gayatri Chakravorty Spivak, "Can the Subaltern Speak?" in Cary Nelson and Lawrence Grossberg, eds., *Marxism and the Interpretation of Culture* (London: Macmillan, 1988).

minority groups themselves and their growing number of supporters. Significant legal and political victories upholding the equal civil
rights of LGBTQ people along with the courageous determination
of increasing numbers of LGBTQ people to be "out" and visible
in society together seem to be slowly turning the tide of public ignorance and fear. However, full social and cultural acceptance of
LGBTQ people will not be achieved by legal and legislative reme-
dies alone. Only when other important social institutions open their
doors to enlightened discussion will some of the final obstacles to
full equality really disappear. Religion remains one of the major
arenas in which ignorance about and hostility toward sexual minorities still dominate many groups. In most of these cases, LGBTQ
people remain abstractions or objects, often portrayed only through
the fantasies of the dominant group itself, rather than real people
who can speak authoritatively about their own lives. Many faith communities continue doggedly to listen only to the characterization of
LGBTQ people proposed by their own heterosexual leaders, assured,
it seems, that no religious or spiritual understanding could possibly
be found within the gay, lesbian, transgender, bisexual, or queer communities themselves. Such an assumption could not be further from
the truth.

The very struggle for dignity in a hostile world, especially a hostile
religious world, has brought with it remarkable religious knowledge
and astonishing spiritual strength to LGBTQ people of faith. LGBTQ
people of faith can be found in every religion, congregation, and faith
community in the world. Because of their lived experience both within
and outside of established communities of faith, LGBTQ people know
what it means to stand courageously for who they are and for what
they believe. They also know how to create and nurture family in
the midst of rejection; how to care for and love friends even through
illness and death; how to hang onto faith, even in the presence of
persistent evil; and how to support each other faithfully and grow
spiritually in the face of hatred and derision. Moreover, they know
the deeply liberating joy of the good news preached to those who are
oppressed, and they know how full of grace an embodied sexuality can
really be. All of these gifts and graces of the spirit and more, all of
this knowledge and strength are desperately needed today, not only

by other marginalized populations, but perhaps even more so by faith communities at large in the dominant culture.

This book series, sponsored jointly by the Center for Lesbian and Gay Studies in Religion and Ministry at Pacific School of Religion and by The Pilgrim Press, is designed precisely to make more widely available the stories, insights, new knowledge and religious gifts of many within the transgender, queer, lesbian, gay, and bisexual communities — not only to support those who might be walking similar paths, but also to awaken the wider religious world to the spiritual genius of people it has all too often denigrated and rejected. For Jews and Christians, after all, there is strong precedent for attending to such people; as Jesus, quoting Psalm 118, pointed out, "The stone that the builders rejected has become the cornerstone" (Mark 12:10). The time has come for faith communities to listen and to learn from new voices and new perspectives.

Cheri DiNovo's engaging look at Christian evangelism is a sparkling example of how the perspectives at the queer margins of society can reimagine central Christian values in ways that are both creative and at the same time deeply faithful to the long tradition of Christian witness. By emphasizing that the church itself needs to be evangelized by those who come from the marginalized outside to challenge the generosity and genuineness of its welcome, DiNovo develops a model of evangelism that undermines the assumptions, methods, and concern for results of current popular teachings on church growth. For DiNovo, evangelism is not about marketing strategies and counting numbers; it is about reenergizing the church to the call of Christ and Christ's extravagant welcome, a call that both questions and "queers" who is the real evangelist, who is the church, and who actually are the outsiders. In this book you will find a truly queer plan for church revitalization, and yes, even church growth, that relies more on the work of the Holy Spirit than on the power of successful marketing. God is at work on and in the margins, if only the mainline church would open its heart to listen, see, and, most of all, learn.

MARY A. TOLBERT
Executive Director
Center for Lesbian and Gay Studies
  in Religion and Ministry
Pacific School of Religion

QU(E)ERYING EVANGELISM

Chapter One

Introduction to Evangelism Outside/In

Called

My own history with the church, like the history of the church in and to which I now minister, is the queer story of the queer action of the Holy Spirit on both the church and me.

The church did not knock on my door. The church did not advertise or proselytize. The church, through a neighbor or friend, did not invite me to church. I, unknowing evangelist, simply knew the United Church to be a church that welcomed queers and therefore might welcome me. I attended church one Sunday not knowing when to stand and when to sit, what Communion meant except that it certainly wasn't a rite open to me, and assuming that I would have to assent to creedal statements that I didn't believe in and to be silent about large parts of my own life and experience. I assumed, in other words, that to become a member of any church, I would have to lie, even in an inclusive church! Looking back, had someone told me that I was the evangelist and the church the object of my evangelism, I would have thought them insane. After all, I barely knew anything about Christianity and even less about church.

Looking back, I would read my story as the story of someone so called by God that her lack of knowledge, her lack of experience, and even her lack of faith could not keep her away. I would share, with she who was me, the stories of Saul/Paul, killer of Christians, and the eunuch in Acts, unclean among Christians, asking Philip for baptism. I would have explained that Saul and the eunuch were evangelists to the early church (Ananias and Philip). Or perhaps I now would welcome she who was me back then: simply and faithfully welcome and listen, which would be enough. And this was in fact what happened to me. And it was enough.

Again

Born into a completely secular household, I was not baptized until my thirties. I had always seen churches as "moral" institutions, meaning judgmental, particularly around matters sexual. A church was the last place I would have ever entered as a young person. Eastern religions seemed much more enthralling, especially in the university. Buddhism didn't have the same reactionary focus as the televangelists I observed while channel surfing. By and large, at that point religion was simply irrelevant to me.

My life began to involve a great deal of death from my teen years on, with most of my biological family dying before I was twenty-one, so I often found myself at funerals. I was horrified to see strangers at funeral homes try to summarize lives that were precious to me. I understood the need to have a ritual around death, but why couldn't it be meaningful? Later, when I took my children to churches for the first time, one of my thoughts was that it would be nice to have the minister actually know the person they were burying. Church involvement might make that possible.

I was also a street kid for most of my teen years and knew what it was to be poor, to be despised. My impression of churches (outside/in) was that they were domains of the middle class, that they were clubs of like minds. Since I had always felt "different" I assumed there was no such club that would want me as a member.

Not until the United Church opened ordination to all its members, including gays and lesbians, did the idea of entering a church present itself as a possibility. Despite my agnostic upbringing, despite my Buddhist interests, there had always been something about the story of Christ's passion that had moved me. I remember thinking that even if his words to the thief at his side were lies, they were still the most beautiful words ever uttered: "Today you will be with me in Paradise" (Luke 23:43). And there was something about the Rolling Stones song about the prodigal son that sent me back to read the parable of the Prodigal Son.[1]

My own life had been about fulfillment in my work and realizing material dreams, and I had done that. By my thirties, I found myself living in a big house with a Mercedes and a swimming pool, yet somehow it all was inadequate. At the heart of it, something was missing; something in me was missing. It was, looking back, a "queer" feeling.

I went to church feeling out of place, and yet I was welcomed. Increasingly what happened at church became the focus of my life. My faith and my understanding of faith deepened. I had been called by Christ but not by anything the church did, except to be welcoming to queers. In looking back, I now see that the one thing my denomination did that allowed me to walk through the doors was to be welcoming to queers. I felt that if they welcomed queers they just might welcome me, queer as I knew in my heart that I was, sinful as I knew I was.

My growth as a Christian was first and foremost a growth in the understanding of my own sinfulness, and a growth in the understanding of my own queerness. By welcoming me, the church mirrored for me the depth of my forgiveness and the depth of God's love. That I might be able to live my life offering the same to others even queerer than myself was and is the greatest gift of all. First of all intellectually intrigued with the idea of Christianity, it then became clear to me that any way of spending my life other than serving this one I was coming to know as Christ would be a waste of time.

My years in seminary were a process of learning, in part, that I might actually be acceptable to my own denomination. Again, I assumed that I would have to lie about who I had been and who I was. I expected everyone to be more "normal" than I was, although I couldn't have really defined what "normal" was. I certainly expected everyone at seminary to be more conversant with Christianity and more "faithful" than I was. As I came to learn more about my denomination and my faith, I came to learn also that it was exactly my

---

1. From the Rolling Stones album, "Beggar's Banquet."

own "difference" that they needed. That they might actually need me: this was a testament to the hospitality and, I would say now, biblical faithfulness of the place.

At seminary I fell in love with the work of the postliberal move-ment, particularly Karl Barth, and then discovered that often those who seemed most theologically rigorous in their work were also, strangely, opposed to the ordination of queers and same-sex marriage. I found and still find friends on both sides of the conservative/liberal church divide. How to speak across the divide? How to uphold *scrip-tura sola* and that scriptural call to hospitality as the ethical imperative, hospitality to the marginalized? How to begin to speak from scripture to scripture, from theology to theology, faithfully as queer? How to bring peace?

Many years and discoveries and books and experiences and studies later, I was "called" to my present inner-city church home. I had wanted to return to the inner city. I was born and grew up in the inner city, so it was familiar to me, and its particular challenges were ones that I thought I was uniquely equipped to handle. I had been a street kid. For most of my life, I was secular and an atheist. I had a lot of energy and was as comfortable with queers (indeed I saw myself as queer) as with those who did not see themselves as queer.

As the woman who in September 2001 came to perform the first legally recognized same-sex marriage in North America[2] and as one always concerned with the survival of my inclusive denomination (the United Church) and inclusive church (Emmanuel Howard Park United), I wanted to "do" anything to guarantee the survival of queers. After all, they had welcomed me! I wanted, I thought, to be all things to all people that some might be saved, to paraphrase Paul. Like other colleagues in inner-city inclusive ministry, I wanted to try all the tech-niques of church growth that emanated from places like Willow Creek Church in Chicago.

---

2. Metropolitan Community Church Toronto performed the first Banns marriage, but this was not recognized legally. The marriage we performed at Emmanuel Howard Park by Banns was registered (by mistake) by the registry office and became the first "legal" marriage, one never rescinded.

Surprisingly, I discovered that not only did the techniques not transfer effectively to our inner-city, queer-positive context, but that they were predicated on a vacuous theology with more in common with colonialism than with scriptural conversion. Clergy and laity who felt like failures because their churches did not grow numerically, and who feared the death of an inclusive Christianity that plagued them, became another group needing evangelism. How to speak faith to them? How to speak faith to ourselves?

That attendance at our evening or morning service grew ceased to be for me the primary question of my or our evangelical ministry. My own struggle with the discipline of being Christian became and is still focused on ignoring those very numbers. To read anything into the numbers that join or attend our church except our ability to be hospitable, I consider a temptation. Our struggle is to be faithful, to be hospitable, to be nonjudgmental. As we succeed in that, we are caught up in evangelism, we are getting out of the way of the Holy Spirit. For us, what is much more significant than the numbers attending is that the queerest among us feel welcomed, and that we can allow ourselves to show our own queerness.

Every time I began to think I understood the movement in which I was caught up, a new concern or question unsettled my complacency. I now have come to understand that this is what the evangelical process looks like.

I came to witness as well as discern that evangelism is a movement and that the movement is from the queerest of those in our area of ministry to ourselves as church. I came to witness as well as discern that evangelism is a movement outside/in. I came to witness as well as discern that the church is the object and not the subject of this movement called evangelism.

We are still waiting for Jesus Christ to arrive. But along the way, and with that expectation, many prophets have made appearances. I particularly highlight two of them in this book, Del and Mary. And I introduce you to some others who, while not transgendered or transsexual, are transgressive, are queer. After all, they are Christian.

Called Back Again

When I came to you brothers and sisters, I did not come proclaiming the mystery of God to you in lofty words or wisdom. For I decided to know nothing among you except Jesus Christ, and him crucified.

(1 Cor. 2:1)

queer 1. strange or odd from a conventional viewpoint; unusually different; singular; *a queer notion of justice.*[3]

A man, flesh and blood, Jewish, is tried, executed, and crucified in first-century Palestine. He has come to be known as Jesus. The followers of his teachings and healings call him the "Christ," the messiah, the anointed one, the son of man and God. His followers claim that he is also the Logos, the Divine Word, and that he overcomes death. His followers claim that he is among us still and that through prayer and discernment he can be heard and followed still. He, both man and divine. He, both alive and dead. What variety of God is this, if not queer?

Feeling out of place myself, with no history of church in my child-hood, I stumbled into a United Church, ostensibly looking for a place where my children could learn the stories of the Bible so that they might one day read Shakespeare more intelligently, looking for a place where I could find purpose in my life. I chose the United Church be-cause of what seemed to me its brave stand to ordain homosexuals who had chosen not to be celibate. Increasingly impressed with the church and gradually called to the ministry, I was followed by one question: "How can we help this church to grow?" I believed then that growing the church, adding people to its pews, was what evange-lism meant. It seemed that the only question that followed from such an understanding was a marketing one.

However, I discovered that the very decision that attracted *me* to the United Church caused many more people to leave.[4] Was that move (to open up ordination to active homosexuals) evangelical even

---

3. *Webster's Unabridged Dictionary of the English Language* (New York: Portland House, 1989).

4. The years 1988–97 saw a loss of 150,000-plus members, but no reliable census was taken regarding why people left. Since the "Community of Concern" initially received the support of 1,000 clergy and more than 2,000 laity one can presume that some of that immediate exodus had something to do with the "issue." Reginald Bibby, *Fragmented Gods: The Poverty and Potential of Religion in Canada* (Toronto: Irwin, 1997), appendix, 376.

if it cost the church membership? If it was, then evangelism had to do with more than attracting numbers. What constituted evangelism?

Two developments assisted my investigation. Queers (meaning lesbians, gays, bisexuals, and transgendered persons) were attending and joining my church (Emmanuel Howard Park), and I began reading and studying the works of several seminal poststructuralists, notably Jacques Derrida and Judith Butler. Paul and other biblical authors began to sound poststructuralist. One could hear Paul in Galatians, "I have been crucified with Christ; and it is no longer I who live, but it is Christ who lives in me" (Gal. 2:20), as referring to the death of the self or the death of the referent or both; "There is no there, there."[5] Or to answer Gertrude, no here/here. Or as Paul says, "May I never boast of anything except the cross of our Lord Jesus Christ, by which the world has been crucified to me, and I to the world" (Gal. 6:14).

It also sounded like a queer (meaning strange, undecipherable, different) starting place, this cross. This "X." This X that erases history, God, self, world, and of course, also births them into being. This X that crosses through but somehow does not erase. This X that might be the rightful starting place for a millennial evangelism. For the same Paul who is no more Paul becomes all things to all people for this crucified one, the One X'd out.

How do we market the undecidable? How do we grow a church among people who haven't read Paul, never mind know that their selves and world have been misplaced? How do we sell a Jesus Christ of questions and questioning and not a Jesus Christ of easy answers? A Jesus Christ who was the worst evangelist in the sense of increasing his following? Jesus Christ, who died with a mere handful of supporters, abandoned, betrayed, ignored, ridiculed? Is evangelism about marketing at all?

In *A History of Christian Missions*, Stephen Neill writes that Christianity has spread in only three ways: colonialism (or Christendom), monasticism, and martyrdom.[6] It was not through cell groups, Matthew parties, discipling, or any other American church growth maneuver.[7] Evangelism when surveyed over the hundreds rather than

---

5. Gertrude Stein, *Portraits and Prayers* (Boston: Beacon Press, 1957), 179.
6. Stephen Neill, *A History of Christian Missions* (London: Penguin, 1984), 57.
7. The work of Bill Hybels, for example. See bibliography.

the tens of years always looks a little different. And, numbers aside, the larger question is: What Christianity are these churches selling? Is it a Christ as presented in scripture? Or a Christ of modernity and fundamentalism?[8]

Poststructuralists are those who question answers. Derrida, rather than adding theory, questioned existing theories. Butler did the same in the area of identity politics, including feminisms. Jesus didn't seem to offer answers either. If he offered anything, it was his very self. Parables, contradictions, and impossible directives were all hallmarks of his ministry.

Both God and not God, Jesus existed on the margins of his world. Both dead and alive somehow, Jesus exists as contradiction, in ours. Christians *are not*, really, either. Christians are those who pray to be Christian but never quite are, except to the non-Christian who maybe notices them only in their moment of crucifixion. Christians are those who are willing to die for what they are not, what is X'd out. To die for what is alive. And yet as we pray for ourselves to attain Christianity, "One must completely abandon any attempt to make something of oneself."[9] How do such persons "do" evangelism? What do they say? Or are they the object of an evangelism that comes from the Other? The Christian, being queer, like the queer (meaning strange or differently sexual), is noticeable for what they (the Christian) are not.

> It is no longer possible to think in our day other than in the void left by man's disappearance. For this void does not create a deficiency; it does not constitute a lacuna that must be filled. It is nothing more, and nothing less, than the unfolding of a space in which it is once more possible to think.[10]

As Christians X'd out, we attempt to give what is not ours to give to those who have already received it. The evangelist tells what they do not know to those who know not, or is told by the Other at the door

---

8. See Bruce B. Lawrence, *Defenders of God* (San Francisco: Harper & Row, 1989) for an argument about the common cause between biblical fundamentalist and modernist agendas, both, as George A. Lindbeck, *The Nature of Doctrine* (Philadelphia: Westminster Press, 1984), would call "propositionalists."

9. Dietrich Bonhoeffer, *The Martyred Christian* (New York: Collier Books, 1983), 174.

10. Michel Foucault, *The Order of Things: An Archaeology of the Human Sciences* (New York: Pantheon, 1971), 342.

what they need to know. Here, perhaps, there is no marketing. Here, perhaps, there is only the actions/nonactions of the Holy Spirit.

Several transgendered persons found a home in our church. Their stories of suffering and exclusion from other places of worship began to become woven into the biblical call from the margins and the shifting nature of those margins that had become a part of ministry in the inner city. Did the self that identified as both man and woman speak somehow of that slippery claim of the Christian? We are both Christian and not Christian. We worship a Jesus alive and dead. We are called to be evangelists and yet we are not evangelists: God/Christ/Holy Spirit is? Given the questioning of foundationalism that emanated from poststructuralism and the qu(e)erying that seemed its method, the "looking again" of poststructuralism became the interesting route.

In the space that Foucault describes as being left, in the space that Jesus the Christ has left for Christians, this thinking starts. One question that emerged early in my thought was, "Am I being obedient?" Not a question a poststructuralist would ask, but certainly a Christian question. Am I being obedient to the Christ of scripture? And of course the answer is always qualified. The Christ is ever and always elusive, and as Christians we must not and cannot speak for Christ but only and ever about Christ. We cannot ever say with surety that we are or are not being obedient. Our actions are, in a sense, actions of resistance. They occur in context, and they change in context.

A member of our evening service attended a rally against a homophobic and racist/sexist group linked to the killing of abortion doctors, yet calling themselves "Christian." She stands as a Christian against them, and also apart from the demonstrators, who wave signs that are anti-Christian. A mainline denominational member stands for the ordination of gays and lesbians *and* over and against the limp liberalism that makes common cause with modernity. Of course Jesus rose from the dead! Owen, a street person, speaks in testimonial style at our Sunday night service and says, "I would not be alive were it not for Jesus Christ." As liberal theologians quest for the Jesus of history, Jesus Christ alive keeps Owen alive. This is not metaphysics. It is a love relationship, as slippery as any between two living beings.

Queer evangelists are obedient in a queer way, always aware of the presence of Christ, always prayerfully following the lead of the present and risen Christ and always humbly cognizant of our own inadequacy before the call. We are aware of the primal lack, the separation between ourselves and God, as keenly as any Orthodox Christian. Truth resides with Christ. Christ is the truth. But it is a truth never fully known in this lifetime. Taylor is correct when he asserts that "When desire forsakes the prospect of complete satisfaction, it opens the possibility of delight."[11] There is the dance of joy but to Golgotha. There are no "answers." There is always the question, the "X" of Christ. For one obedient, liberation of any kind must also be qu(e)eried as Halperin does when speaking of the gay liberation movement, "Sexual liberation may have liberated our sexuality but it has not liberated us *from* our sexuality; if anything it has enslaved us more profoundly to it."[12]

The more I learned, the more I unlearned. If Christ is alive, then the question about Christ can never be answered unless Christ comes to answer it. What became interesting was the listening and the enquiry itself. A theology of listening and enquiry drew me to the methodology of the case study. What if scripture pointed us back to listening to our neighbor as it seemed to do? What if the margins continue to speak to us as church and to us as unchurched?

Evangelism certainly did not seem to be about bigger congregations or more self-identified Christians. Instead, I came back to the notion of obedience to the One who calls as being the motivation. And because we, being obedient, are called by the One called Christ to love, I wondered at the fear of the shifting grounds of postmodernisms when the New Testament itself offered no sure thing but only various "takes" on Jesus/Christ.[13] I read quotes like, "Over against postmodern masturbatory language games, this kind of transformational epistemological stewardship attempts to construct an alternative consciousness, an alternative worldview that will bear fruit in the healing of all creation,"[14] for example. I wondered if the oft-expressed fear of "relativism" was

---

11. Mark C. Taylor, *Erring: A Postmodern A/Theology* (Chicago: University of Chicago Press, 1987), 152.

12. Ibid., 20.

13. Raymond E. Brown, *The Churches the Apostles Left Behind* (New York: Paulist Press, 1984), and others as examples of the different "Jesus" of the different testaments.

14. J. Richard Middleton and Brian J. Walsh, *Truth Is Stranger Than It Used to Be* (Downers Grove, Ill.: InterVarsity Press), 171.

not just another dinner with the devil of modernity. Creation *will not* be healed by us. Surely, scripturally, seeing ourselves as the healers of creation or of anything else is setting ourselves up as gods. Finally we must admit that we can do no good deeds, that this is God's world.

Original lack/sin is finally the opportunity for Christian compassion. The wounds of X are ours, and we, bleeding, can *then and only then* see the wounds of the other. The enemy of queerness is morality. Where flowery words and romantic sentiments mask the terror of death, queers assert with Bonhoeffer, "Death is the supreme festival on the road to freedom."[15] Or the necessity for a new understanding of morality that judges not. A "looking again" through queer eyes and listening to the neighbor with queer ears always expecting to hear the unexpected, the shocking. The operative ethic is humility.

In a sense, fundamentalism and secularity are bedfellows. As closed systems, both disallow the miraculous, the mind changing, the stranger at the door, the return of Christ. Fundamentalism knows. Newtonian science knows. As Roof and McKinney surmise, the mainline liberal church has spawned secularity and fundamentalism by an embrace of nineteenth-century science and its attempts to finally understand. Queerness does not know; it questions. It is ready for anything, ever anticipating the messenger with a message. Meanwhile, on behalf of the strange one at the door there are actions to be taken. The strange and possibly angelic must be protected if we, attempting to be faithful to hope, are to hear their message. As Foucault said:

> If I don't say what must be done, it isn't because I believe that there's nothing to be done. On the contrary, it is because I think there are a thousand things to do, to invent, to forge, on the part of those who, recognizing the relations of power in which they're implicated have decided to resist or escape them.[16]

If the Bible is a metanarrative, it is a prestructural one. Many voices raise praises to the many faces of God in many, often contradictory, ways. Jesus speaks God in a new way. Exegesis and midrash exist within the text itself undoing and redoing what went before. Looking at scripture queerly requires only reading the words the way a child

---

15. Bonhoeffer, *The Martyred Christian*, 212.
16. Michel Foucault, *Remarks on Marx: Conversations with Ducio Trombadori*, trans. R. James Goldstein and James Cascaito (New York: Semiotext[e], 1991), 174.

might, as words that tell a story. However both author/Author and subject/Christ are absent from this strange text. It writes us surely, but as divine milieu it also is crucified and reborn. There is nothing structural about Christ. X slips as easily from the grasp of canon as from ours, and yet is unknowable without it. The Bible breathes more surely than we do.

But what of evangelism? I came to see that this process of listening to the neighbor speaking from the margins and reading the story queerly might *be* evangelism. I might learn something. I might be changed. I might be claimed as Christ's. I might also be the object of the movement of evangelism and then its subject.

This *might be* evangelism and unabashed apologetics. Apologetics is faith being absorbed into unfaith. Because we are called, as Paul was too, to be fools to Greeks still. Why apologize? Because as Levinas says:

> Not to philosophize is still to philosophize. The philosophical discourse of the West claims the amplitude of an all encompassing structure or of an ultimate comprehension. It compels every other discourse to justify itself before philosophy.[17]

And this bully, philosophy, that insists that we make sense has now allowed within its ranks a sense of sense that is sounding increasingly theological. The Christ that I found as I began this study calling from outside the church door might also call to us from theorists and philosophers, themselves quite queer. There is a conversation to be had.

Also, those like Butler and Derrida and others have done some of our work for us (and better than we) in clearing away the Enlightenment and what Luther would call "whore reason."[18] Levinas, for example, is more supportive of a transcendent God as the definer of "immanence" than most postliberal neoorthodox.[19] Of course, for a Christian, this is still not Christian.

---

17. Emmanuel Levinas, *Otherwise Than Being, or Beyond Essence*, trans. Alphonso Lingis (Dordrecht: Martinus Nijhoff, 1981), 153.

18. Brian Gerrish, *Grace and Reason: A Study in the Theology of Luther* (Oxford: Oxford University Press, 1962), 168.

19. This is also the case with comparison to the boundedness and rationalism of some postliberal theological writing (i.e., George A. Lindbeck), where any attempts at arguing ontologically are muffled.

Queer Christians will "be all things to all people" (1 Cor. 9:22) because we must. In every context in which the obediently, resistantly queer Christian finds herself or himself, we are called to speak of our love, especially to those who "... find themselves implicated in power relationships they decide to resist."[20] This will, of course, be contextual, and we will, of course, fail.

A member of our congregation found herself being marginalized as a Christian in a feminist collective and so defends Christianity. The same woman found herself marginalized as a woman in an all-male Christian forum and so defends feminism.

So, I found myself attempting to be obedient and failing, attempting to listen to the margins and failing, attempting to hear Christ even in theorists and failing. And yet perhaps I was also succeeding by way of this beautiful failure in coming closer to evangelism theologically, closer to that One of whom Galatians speaks. "There is no longer Jew or Greek, there is neither male or female; for all of you are one in Christ Jesus" (Gal. 3:28). All meaning just that: all.

What if all meant all? What if difference and alterity were built into the very heart of God? What if that is just another way of upholding the Trinity? What if the incarnation means that Christ is alive and can be found at the doors of the church? What if listening to the good news is as important as preaching the good news? What if we will never find any answers to any of our questions and learn to love questioning as though that were the answer? What if that is what we mean when we say that Christ is the answer? What if the transgendered/transsexual person is a reflection of all of us and a clearer reflection of Christ? What if queer is a continuum understood in context as absorbing all? What if it is at our very queerest that we are evangelical/faithful and that in its hospitality to the very queerest that the church is at its most faithful/evangelical? What if the ones who seemed the most strange, sexually different (queer) at Emmanuel Howard Park had the most to teach us, the church?

How then do we act? How do we evangelize? The answer, simply is, *we* don't. The Holy Spirit does, through us or to us, in answer to the call of Christ (X). The better question is, how do *we* get out of the

---

20. Foucault, *Remarks on Marx*.

way? How do we allow the reign of God to show itself to the neighbor? Certainly not through the violence we would inflict by telling them we know better than they.

We act because we must. Levinas again:

> But responsibility for another comes from what is prior to my freedom. It does not come from the time made up of presences, nor presences that have sunk into the past and are representable, the time of beginnings or assumings. It does not allow me to constitute myself into an *I think* substantial like a stone, or, like a heart of stone, existing in and for oneself. It ends up in substitution for another, in the condition — or the unconditionality of being a hostage. Such responsibility does not give one time, a present for recollection or coming back to oneself; it makes one always late. Before the neighbor I am summoned and do not just appear, from the first I am answering to an assignation.[21]

The reign of God is not the calendar future. It is scriptural history from which we live a postmessianic existence. In the crucifixion and resurrection of Jesus Christ, history has reached its end. We live there. But what do we do? How do we know what to do? Queer followers of a queer God proceed evangelically sure of failure, guaranteed of success, to the cross where all are crucified. They do this prayerfully, praying not for the healing of a few, but for all those who will not or cannot be healed. And knowing that prayer is never a priori but always a posteriori, after the text. Prayer is uttered from the Cross.

Prayerfully, the queer Christian prays to understand the activities of Christ in any place, at any time. Then we follow. In Christianity the Christ *is alive.* There is still no achievement possible, no more than falling in love can be claimed as an achievement. And no disputing the love affair. And no disputing that the queer Christian will defend the beloved. We meet the beloved in the queer other; to love the other is to love that which is queer in us.

Here there are no spiritual "heights," no informing experience, no "wow." There are instead the shared spiritual depths, and words, always words, and always the Word first.

But what about the church? The church, the body of Christ (X), understood in its queerness, does not exist from the other or the Other. It exists to give itself away to the other, for the other. It does not exist

---

21. Levinas, *Otherwise Than Being*, 160.

to take from the other for its own agenda. This church of Christ exists to martyr itself. What does this mean? The evangelical church exists to die. This also is evangelism. This news is food to the one who hungers. To the one who is homeless, it is a home. To the one alone, it is community. To the one dying, it is life. Perhaps this is the martyrdom of which Neill spoke.

Perhaps better than any Christian explanation of the conversion moment is Levinas's:

> It is a passivity or a passion in which desire can be recognized, in which the *"more in the less"* awakens in its most ardent, noblest, and most ancient flame a thought given over to thinking more than it thinks. But this desire is of another order than the desires involved in hedonist or eudaemonist affectivity or activity, where the desire is invested, reached, and identified as an object of need.[22]

Its origin is not ours but (to a Christian) Christ's. It is in conversion (meaning to converse, to dialogue, or to be the opposite) or in the mirror of the other that we see ourselves the opposite of the true human. It is the moment in which we discover how far from Christ we are, how far from human. That most human moment, when we *see* as if for the first time, is a moment of humiliation and exaltation. To *hear* the call and to *see* ourselves.

How does it happen? When Christ is ready, not when we are. Where the Holy Spirit is and not where we are. This is not a game. There is no winning or losing here. There is simply and gloriously grace. Not that we are nothing: we are the beloved ones and we attempt obedience, so we preach and we act for we must in every minute say, " Thank you!" What else could we do, we who are queerly Christian?

•

And so I found myself in the company of the evangelizing church. That is where the story began. Right or wrong, I thought it might be a good thing to "grow" this church that had become home to me. Then I reread scripture with queer eyes. There I discovered that this phenomenon called evangelism had little to do with growth. Queers came

---

22. Ibid.

in the doors of the sanctuary, and we were invitational. They taught us how to be hospitable. They became us. New queerness arrived. We had a story to share as well. As if to embarrass us, the church grew numerically. It became obvious that everyone knew themselves on some level to be queer. We prayed. That's how it all began

There were to follow so many qu(e)eries, about queer, about inclusivity, about morality and ethicality, about church growth and evangelism and about church itself. We needed to begin somewhere, but where?

Beginning Again?

Where else to begin, but here? When else, but now? As many clergy find themselves, I found myself as a theology student thinking I could make a difference in the way evangelism was "done." I started an evening service in a downtown church, presiding in blue jeans, backed by a rhythm and blues band, quoting Kurt Cobain. As a member of a statedly inclusive denomination that would and did ordain openly gay and lesbian candidates, I thought the only reason people stayed away from churches had to do with the "way" the gospel was "packaged and sold."

I believed that if we created a church that was user friendly, all those who hungered for spirituality and spent millions on the new age would come rushing back. My hope was a church in the "round," as Letty Russell described it.[23] My denomination was supportive and was already doing most of the "right things" (although I thought an updated "look" was needed). Our first service was a moderate success, after weeks of buildup and postering and public relations spots. The novelty soon wore off, and we settled into a service for twenty or so faithful who mostly came to hear the band.

Many years and many experiments and many seminars, books, and conferences on church growth later, I slowly became aware that evangelism might not have to do with numerical growth at all.

In particular, the issue that had cost our own denomination members was that of the ordination of gays and lesbians. The only church

---

23. Letty M. Russell, *Church in the Round* (Louisville: Westminster John Knox, 1993).

that was open at that time to the ordination of gays and lesbians was the church specifically founded for them, Metropolitan Community Church. Was there something about the "queer" issue that challenged Christians in a unique way? Was there something about the "queer" issue that called us back to a greater faithfulness at the cost of members? What had this to do with evangelism?

I witnessed many leaders of inclusive inner-city churches struggling to accommodate their church councils' (and their own) desire for numerical growth. Many experimented with alternative services, small-group ministries, outreach of various sorts. Many crowded the conferences of visiting clergy from the megachurches, the stars of the church growth movement, went home, and tried to replicate the formulas. Lost in the process seemed to be any real excitement around investigating what our call to be evangelists might really mean. Where was the theory? Where was the theology? Why were we frantically trying to fill pews anyway?

Meanwhile, I had become seduced by the exciting thought sweeping continental Europe that seemed to mesh so nicely with Christian theology. Philosophy had been questioning "giving" and "colonialism" as well as its own assumptions. Far more exciting than gatherings dedicated to church growth were the conferences I attended on "Postmodernism and Religion" where philosophers and theologians spoke to each other and (astoundingly) university students listened.

Perhaps philosophers had something to say to Christians and vice versa. Perhaps queer theorists had something to say to Christians and vice versa!

The paradox was that despite giving up on most church growth material, my congregation was beginning to grow numerically. I began to describe my role as "getting out of the way of the Spirit," which was far more proactive than it sounded. I began to wonder if the foundation of the "marketing of the gospel" movement was not, in fact, a sort of lack of faith in the very gospel they were attempting to buy and sell.

This I also began to think of as "queer evangelism." Queer, because it was inclusive of queers (lesbigays and transgendered persons). Queer, because it happened despite all our efforts and had nothing to do with numbers. Queer, because it posited a church which while siding with the marginalized became marginalized. Queer, because this produced a very different church with very different people than the suburban megachurches represented. Queer, because it was based on a theology which was far from solid, creedal, or closed and yet remained profoundly orthodox. Queer, because it represented an evangelism from the outside in, from the queer (different, marginalized, other) fringes.

By feeding people and offering a service which spoke to the needs of the sexually and socially marginalized, our congregation effectively doubled in number in two years. Sardonically, however, I noted that the marginalized were often not considered to constitute the real "growth" of the church because few were financially contributing.

Quickly I lost interest in church growth and gained interest in evangelism. Then I met Del.

Del seemed to me an apt example of the target of this evangelism, of perhaps a new church. Or perhaps Del was the new evangelist and our church was the target of her evangelical efforts.

Del felt marginalized everywhere. First and foremost in the Roman Church in which she had been raised because they considered her transgender status and bisexuality a "sin," to quote Del. Second, because she felt rejected by some in the gay and lesbian community who considered Del either too male to be female or too "weird" to be male.[24] Del came because she was physically hungry and we offered a free dinner. Del stayed and eventually became a "staff" person because our church became home. How and why that happened and how and why Del chose our church and not some other church became the focus of my interest.

Surprisingly, when qu(e)eried others who were more typical church attenders (heterosexual, married, parents) also had felt queer (unaccepted, different, marginalized) in relation to other churches. Caring about the church being a home for someone like Del was also caring about the church being a home for them.

The church's call to the marginalized, which Del and people like Del came to represent — yet not just the transgendered person but all

---

24. Conversation, February 10, 2001.

who had felt unaccepted (queer) — seemed to challenge not only our praxis but our theological basis, or perhaps to simply call us back, as so often happens, to our biblical roots.

I like to think that what happened over this long journey was, for me, an evangelization, an evangelization from the marginalized *to* our church and *to* me, a movement of the Holy Spirit with or without us.

Chapter Two

Models and Mentors

Beginning with Mentors

Excited by the possibility of growing an inclusive, seeker-sensitive church using all my skills as a former business owner, I initially looked to those American examples of what at the time I understood to be church success. Two came immediately to mind: Willow Creek Community Church, in the suburbs of Chicago, because of their aggressive and continuous marketing to pastors like me (I received monthly invitations to church growth seminars, publications, etc.), and Riverside Church in New York City because of its combination of "success" and social justice.

Willow Creek Community Church was founded in 1975, and almost immediately half its weekly budget was spent on media and promotion. With over two thousand members, fifteen thousand or so "guests" every weekend, and five hundred baptisms a year, it stood among the giants of megachurches.[1] There were others, of course, such as Saddleback, Crystal Cathedral, and Houston's Second Baptist, but as an inner-city northerner I certainly heard about Willow Creek more.

My early forays into the evangelical discourse were theologically nonquestioning. It seemed to me on a cursory reading of the New Testament that we were called to "grow" the church by none other than Christ himself. Although I had been trained in my tradition not to proof text, the seminal and only passage that reverberated in me was Jesus calling us to "go therefore and make disciples of all the nations" (Matt. 28:19). I didn't question what a "disciple" was and what this act of baptism entailed, but it seemed to intimate that the task of growing the church was critical (certainly for the church as institution this seemed so).

---

1. *www.willowcreek.org/faq/evangelism-query.html.*

34

If anything I was appalled at the lack of interest in the vital ministry of "keeping the church alive" in my mainline denomination. I consumed books about the "how-tos" of church growth. I read Lyle Schaller, for example. In his book, *Innovations in Ministry Models for the 21st Century*, a pretty typical church growth manual, the clarion call that growth is the aim seems implicit as well as explicit.

> While some may deplore the "consumerism" of this era, the generations born after 1955 are forcing the churches to be more sensitive to the religious needs of people. As the churches respond, new forms of ministry are being created. Another result is that new records in church attendance in American Protestantism are being set year after year. To be more precise, the number of people worshipping in Protestant churches on the typical weekend in 1993 was larger than the total in 1953 or 1973 or 1983.[2]

Not only is "growth" here understood as being unquestionably good, but even the data seems out of sync with other analysts who see the glass as half empty (see Bibby's research again).

George Hunter III, in *How to Reach Secular People,* compares the challenge to football:

> While Christendom is gone with the wind and the Church no longer has the home field advantage, a growing number of Christian groups and churches are becoming like the Notre Dame football team — who relish the challenge of playing the game on the other team's field! . . . To be sure, the challenge Christians face in a secular world is more serious than anything Notre Dame ever faces in the Orange Bowl. We are called to mission in a fallen world, whose kingdoms are not yet the Kingdom of our God and of Christ. . . . [3]

Christ as quarterback in a war with secularity contrasts sharply with the bleeding, tortured, pacifist participant in the crucifixion, doesn't he?

William Easum, in *How to Reach Baby Boomers*, insists that churches can accomplish these changes without abandoning any of the basic tenets of Christianity as defined by the various denominations. Nor do these changes dilute the basic substance of Christianity. But these

---

2. Lyle E. Schaller, *Innovations in Ministry: Models for the 21st Century* (Nashville: Abingdon Press, 1994), 12.

3. George G. Hunter III, *How to Reach Secular People* (Nashville: Abingdon Press, 1992), 171.

changes do significantly alter the manner in which pastors and laity proclaim, package, market, and give leadership to the good news.[4] In other words the product, Christianity, is unquestioned and simply assumed; it is to the packaging that the focus has moved.

While reading I realized that the more interesting questions for church growth enthusiasts might be ones never discussed: Why did the nineties see such an increase in the focus on church growth? Why were clergy and laity flocking to the new gurus of "how" instead of the theologians wrestling with the "why"? What was everyone so frightened of anyway? What wasn't working that sent them (and myself) scrambling for assistance in churches around the world?

As the decade proceeded, the books I read seemed to become less and less interested in any theological discussion at all and more and more interested in marketing pure and simple. In *Natural Church Development*, Christian A. Schwartz and Christoph Schalk, masters of church planting, develop a vocabulary that speaks this new language with no apologies: "growth automisms, eight quality characteristics, biotic principles, spiritualizing and technocratic paradigms, principle-oriented versus model-oriented approach, minimum strategy, the 65 hypothesis...."[5]

Thanks to church growth gurus such as these, by the end of the nineties evangelism sounded like a science or at least a well-honed and understood business strategy. Natural church development became a business in its own right, as did the Alban Institute and others.

As church folk we could buy answers to all our questions about how to change our (assumed) dying, nineteenth-century, Luddite, seeker-insensitive, bureaucratically stymied, liturgically boring museums of religion into exciting worshipful, technologically advanced, twenty-first-century, thriving theaters that would draw scores of the spiritually hungry. And all we had to do was buy or study this "system" or this "program" or this "book." Most of them had good ideas, usable techniques, and of course, most excitingly, success stories, "before and afters." Capitalism could improve Christianity, or there was something

---

4. William Easum, *How to Reach Baby Boomers* (Nashville: Abingdon Press, 1991), 20.

5. Christian A. Schwartz and Christoph Schalk, *Implementation Guide to Natural Church Development* (Carol Stream, Ill.: ChurchSmart Resources, 1998), 7.

biblical about capitalism, we were told. Wasn't the early church a sort of pyramid sales scheme? Wasn't it an example of expert marketing?

I wondered how this would all sound to the martyrs.

Although these manuals were filled with lines from scripture, the fact that churches needed or indeed should grow was never questioned. To my understanding, questions of postcolonialism, imperialism, or the very use of the marketing and management techniques of capitalism were never posed.

I noticed as I experimented on and with my congregants that anxieties began to arise. As host of a multifaith campus radio show called *The Radical Reverend* (radical because Christian, I said when asked) I regularly worked with persons of other faiths. They began to look like potential converts. Was that my purpose with them? My associates, my secular friends, even my own family, all began to look like "potential customers" or "leads," as they would have been called in my business. Attending a Bill Hybels Willow Creek Church symposium on church growth in Toronto felt little different than attending the sales conferences back when I had had my own personnel firm. In fact, weren't we simply headhunters of a different sort? I remember the term "trophies of grace" used when describing new converts.[6] I went home and looked at my sales trophies from my business days and tried to think Christ. It didn't compute.

Other anxieties were in evidence as well. Although my colleagues in other congregations and I were trying to start cell groups and experiment with marketing, advertising, and all of the myriad techniques of all the myriad books, little of it actually worked. Ultimately it seemed to hinge more on the charisma of the minister, the geographical placement of the church (suburban congregations expanded, inner-city congregations didn't), and the sheer effort of a core of committed individuals.

This information was anecdotal, of course, but everywhere and certainly for the mainline denominations both in Canada and in the States, the overall figures seemed to bear this out. As Bibby's work progressed, the slight and recent overall growth, for example, could

---

6. Queensway Cathedral, Toronto, 1999.

as easily be explained by demography as the church growth movement.[7] The total number of Protestant Christians in North America
didn't seem to grow much, just redistribute geographically from time
to time.

More important, it all seemed to be about "our" effort, even though
God was credited with any success. If God was behind the growth,
then why did we all have to work so hard? Wasn't this "works
righteousness," I began to ask.

Conservative evangelicals even questioned Willow Creek Community Church's own self assessment. G. A. Pritchard, in a work entitled
Willow Creek Seeker Services, challenged the claims. He described fewer
than 15 percent of Willow Creek's converts as true seekers, finding instead that they were simply Christians switching churches. He looked
critically at their "application of marketing and management methods
to Christianity."[8]

The other question that kept arising in discussions about Willow
Creek Community Church and the model for growth that it offered
was the theology espoused. What was one expected to believe in order
to become a "trophy of grace"? Although the core beliefs espoused on
its Web site lead to more questions than answers, what I noted was
the similarity in views about moral topics. Abortion was "an unacceptable solution to the problem of unwanted pregnancy."[9] Homosexuality
was "not God's design for relationship."[10] The theological center of
Willow Creek Community Church seemed little different from the
mainstream. It certainly was not queer positive. No matter how welcoming it said it was to women, it certainly read the Bible through
a patriarchal lens. I'd suggest that the Bible's primacy is the opening of discussion, not the last word, on any Christian ethical issues.[11]
So were they simply dressing up mainstream exclusive theology in a
welcoming guise?

---

7. See the Bibby texts cited in this work.
8. G. A. Pritchard, *Willow Creek Seeker Services* (Grand Rapids, Mich.: Baker Books,
1994), 797.
9. *www.willowcreek.org.*
10. Ibid.
11. One of the exercises I had our confirmands at Emmanuel Howard Park do was to attempt
to find any references to abortion in the Bible. There aren't any. Clearly, even "Thou shalt not
kill" was also understood and is still understood by many in faith as not universally prescriptive.

After all, it was true that queers, even trans folk, were welcomed in evangelical and conservative churches — with the hope of transforming them into straight, non-trans folk. As Christianity historically encountered difference, the meeting usually ended in the colonization of the other. Was Willow Creek colonizing or was it Christian?

In searching for church models and mentors, we also discovered another example, a church that although large (around twenty-five hundred at regular Sunday worship) had achieved that status in a very different way. Riverside Church New York had a history of brave social justice stands (pacifism even during the Second World War, for example) and had become inclusive, interracial, and even interdenominational while still at least maintaining numbers. It boasted a restaurant, book store, banks of elevators, multiple small groups, and ministries.[12] What was its history? How had it maintained its preeminence in the liberal church world?

Our confirmation group and some parents accompanied me on an exchange trip with Riverside youth. We gawked at the immensity of the cathedral modeled on Chartres. We laughed in delight at our view of the Hudson River from the eighteenth floor where we stayed. We were astounded as we heard Rev. Dr. James Forbes caution that if any of his congregants stayed away on the Gay Pride Sunday when the marchers from Riverside were to be commissioned, that they would need a "doctor's note."[13] We noted that around 60 percent of the congregation was African American and that James Forbes, himself African American, put the lie to the racist stereotype of African Americans as homophobic. We could not believe that this was a congregation that was both United Church of Christ *and* American Baptist! How could one congregation cross that seemingly immense divide? Even their liturgy was a stirring mix of gospel and traditional church music, step dancing and classical. We described it back home as if we were Muslims and had been to Mecca! A large, secure, unafraid church could be inclusive, welcoming, built on a questioning theological basis. It could be a mix of a divergent community of difference.

---

12. Peter J. Paris et al., *The History of the Riverside Church in the City of New York* (New York: New York University Press, 2004).

13. Sunday worship, June 27, 2004.

The Riverside Church is the world's most prominent institutionaliza-
tion of Protestant liberalism. Most important, it is a church that was
built in the midst of the fundamentalist-modernist debate over the
infallible inspiration of the Bible, a debate that engulfed the Protestant churches from the early 1920s until the present day. This church
emerged out of the mutual vision of John D. Rockefeller Jr. and Harry
Emerson Fosdick, a collaborative venture between one of America's
greatest philanthropists and its most renowned liberal preacher.[14]

So says Peter Paris. But perhaps Riverside could be read differently.
What we diaspora Christians witnessed was a "welcoming" place, a
place that practiced "hospitality" in the deepest sense and therefore
could be called biblically orthodox if not literalist. Difference had
been bred in the bone of Riverside with the amalgamation of capitalism (Rockefeller Jr.) and pacifism (Fosdick), with the wedding of the
Baptist and United churches.

Inclusiveness that could witness Fidel Castro as preacher standing
in a nave built with Rockefeller dollars was inclusive indeed. It was no
surprise to us that, like ours, Riverside was the first church in its country to welcome their brothers and sisters from other faiths to worship
after September 11, 2001. PBS filmed a documentary entitled "America in Healing at Riverside Church," a service of mourning including
Buddhists, Jewish, and Muslim clergy.[15]

Riverside's mission statement of 1992 heralded a very different
megachurch from the one encountered at Willow Creek:

> The Riverside Church commits itself to welcoming all persons, celebrat-
> ing the diversity found in a congregation broadly inclusive of persons
> from different backgrounds of race, culture, ethnicity, gender, age and
> sexual orientation. Members are called to a spiritual quality of life in-
> dividually and collectively and to personal and social transformation
> that witness to God's saving purposes for all creation. Therefore, the
> Riverside Church pledges itself to action, reflection and education for
> peace and justice, the realization of the vision of the heavenly banquet
> where all are loved and blessed.[16]

The humility of witness rather than teaching, welcoming rather
than discipling, hospitality rather than judgment or morality leaves

---

14. Paris, *History of the Riverside Church*, 1.
15. Ibid., 3.
16. Ibid., 4.

that space that Foucault speaks of, a space where peace and justice might occur.

It is humility after all that is evident in the new philosophical discourse:

> Archaeological — and not transcendental — in the sense that it will not seek to identify the universal structures of all knowledge or of all possible moral action, but will seek to treat the instances of discourse that articulate what we think, say and do as so many historical events. And this critique will be genealogical in the sense that it will not deduce from the form of what we are what it is impossible for us to do and know, but it will separate out, from the contingency that has made us what we are, the possibility of no longer being, doing or thinking what we are, do, or think. It is not seeking to make possible a metaphysics that has finally become a science; it is seeking to give new impetus, as far and wide as possible, to the undefined work of freedom.[17]

Such a place where freedom is possible is also inevitably chaotic. William Sloane Coffin was no stranger to dissent when he arrived at Riverside in 1977, but even he experienced the unexpected:

> I asked Laubach after I got here when I was being driven out of my mind by lack of structure; I said, "How come this place is so chaotic?" He said, "Because it's Baptist. Because there's no organization. There's too much organization." It's a very good answer. There's not a nice Presbyterian structure, Anglican structure, Methodist structure. There's no kind of structure. So there's too much structure. Two boards? That's crazy. And then there's no clear understanding of what's staff and what's board. And there's no very clear understanding of what kind of respect and authority is due to an ordained person.[18]

The miracle is that Riverside has survived. Although over two thousand people take part in its weekly worship and many distinct ministries and congregations exist within its Cathedral-like structure, it is not a miracle of growth. In fact, attendance has ebbed and flowed, and remained more or less stable over the years (which by growth standards would speak more to a decrease). Controversy and dissension, rifts and splits, all have happened, and yet it remains an inner-city

---

17. Michel Foucault, "What Is Enlightenment?" *The Foucault Reader*, ed. Paul Rabinow (New York: Pantheon Books, 1984), 46.

18. Paris, *History of the Riverside Church*, 47.

church committed to inclusion. One could argue that even their theology is inclusive, which is to say, they are open to many variations of
theological opinion and thought.

Gene Laubach commented, "I've sent three children out from this
church who try in vain to repeat it. I know the Riverside theology
exists because in spite of all the crap that you experience here, there
is also something that is so powerful that you want to repeat this
when you get away." Riverside's enduring theology of culture might
be summed up with a question, "Is anything secular?" For three quarters of a century Riversiders have by their actions and their words
answered with a resounding no. In successive religious climates of fear
of being characterized as "not Christian," or later fear of decline, other
liberal Protestant institutions have chosen to avoid dealing with fundamentalism, poverty, race, sexuality, nuclear defense, immigration,
and other faiths. This is not to suggest that everything is acceptable
to the Riverside theology. Things may be imperfect, corrupt, unjust,
unpleasant, or simply unaesthetic, and the prophetic preaching of the
Riverside pulpit testifies to the enduring faith in God met in culture by answering the question "Who We Are" with the "the three
Is.... We are an interdenominational, interracial, and international
congregation." At Riverside, the liberal ideal of inclusion still lives.[19]

The failure (and success) of Riverside to be all things to all people is,
in a sense, a most glorious failure. It is the biblical failure (and success)
of the early church of Acts that ended in an enduring legacy and the
death of most of its members. The Christ of Riverside is different,
elusive, undefinable, and yes, queer. So queer that homophobe and
queer sit (however uncomfortably) side by side.

The conclusion of our wonderful weekend saw our little crew energized, excited, and ready to re-create what we had seen back home.
That's always where the trouble begins.

Back Home: Beginning

It was both thrilling and depressing to witness Riverside at work and
worship for an inner-city minister like me pastoring in a church with

---

19. Ibid., 51.

around 120 at worship, a budget that was still far from breaking even, and a worship team that had few resources because money was so scarce.

The incredibly hard work of a team of committed laity and the marathon weeks attesting to my own labor had grown our church. That was obvious. It was also obvious that the early rush of excitement and new faces had settled in to a kind of plateau of attendance. Our numbers hadn't budged much for a year despite all our efforts to implement techniques we had learned.

We didn't have a Rockefeller as patron; in fact, we had very few middle-class or professional congregants. We had a (slowly) growing evening service of the poor and a (slowly) growing morning service of the working class. Money was better, but it wasn't good enough to afford the sort of high-profile guest preachers or performers that had made our experience of worship at Riverside so joyful and awe inspiring.

I humbly recognized that although I was confident as a preacher, and received accolades from congregants, I also wasn't that rare charismatic individual who attracts crowds simply because of their God-given gifts. I was, like many of my colleagues, simply doing my best. My best, after Riverside, didn't seem good enough.

Our team of exceptional laity who had, for several years since my arrival, worked so diligently began to exhibit signs of fatigue. A few events we had planned failed in rather monumental ways. Despite all our promotional and advertising efforts, a noted gay and "out" high-profile politician who spoke on same-sex marriage drew a smaller crowd than we had at regular Sunday worship. That the Ontario Supreme Court had ruled same-sex marriage legal a few days before didn't help since the issue for Ontarians, anyway, seemed to be over. The organizer, an exceptionally faithful and hard-working congregant, quipped, "We couldn't fill this sanctuary even if Christ came back!"

We booked a well-known children's performer only to have him not show up on the day of the concert! An arts festival saw only the actual arts exhibitors show up, again despite all our efforts to market and promote. Our anxiety was beginning to include the nagging doubt that not only were all our efforts in vain, but that clearly even God didn't want to see our church survive.

Added to our concerns, the usual politics and personalities of congregational life seemed to challenge even our modest gains in membership and attendance. As we developed a higher profile as a queer-positive church, we lost members who either were vocal in their disagreement or left quietly without saying much. Often when asked, they'd cite some other concern, knowing how I felt about the issue, but we suspected the increasing presence of queers and the poor made them feel uncomfortable. One former member suggested that it was no longer a safe place for children. I countered that most abuse to children happened with those the children knew, not with someone the children met at church who might suffer from mental illness, but we also implemented new procedures so that as much as possible our children would be guaranteed safety. We lost that family anyway. Every loss felt like the ultimate failure. We grieved them all.

We lost members to death as well. For our poor who suffered from mental illness and addiction, life expectancy wasn't good, but as church we hoped that we could somehow, in prayer and with God's help, keep our members alive. Sadly, horribly, we realized we could provide family, food, and love, and we might change lives dramatically, but we were not God. The funerals that we performed and attended also felt like failures. Our church was still small enough that the metaphor of family was different than in the megachurches, even Riverside. It seemed to those of us who had come from secularity that church membership also increased our suffering. We were loving more and losing more. It hurt.

From more than one congregant I heard how hard it was to be a member of our church, how challenging it could be. I felt the same way. The occasional offer to apply for a clergy position at a suburban church with a healthy budget and a lot of congregants began to sound enticing to me. We were exhausted. Was trying to grow a church that was welcoming to queers using church growth techniques possible?

We began to question the question. Del, our transgendered music director, with her usual wit and wisdom said it best: "It all becomes much easier when you just give up."

At some point, we put down the books on technique and method and set aside the focus on growth. It wasn't working for us anyway. We weren't increasing in faith using that strategy; we were only increasing in anxiety. I believe, looking back, that subtly but profoundly, through suffering and losing, like Christians before us, we returned to scripture, to the cross, and away from the culture. After all, in scripture, the last word on the church was one of dissolution and loss. The cross, then the martyrs, then the horror of Revelation. The good news was that the last word in scripture was, so to speak, God's and not ours. As Del had said, on some level, not perhaps at first even consciously, we "just gave up."

One of our other members struggling with addiction also pointed the way, queer evangelist that he was, when he said, "The first step is to admit that you are powerless." I recognized my addiction to church growth theory and church growth itself. From there on in, all I or we could do was what we were called to do: be welcoming to the marginalized. We had hit bottom, in the twelve-step lexicon. It was time to qu(e)ery everything we thought we knew about evangelism.

Beginning: The History of My Approach

As I lived and relived my questions around evangelism, other lived questions approached me as minister. Various individuals, attracted perhaps by the something queer (different, strange) in me, sought my counsel. I became involved with their questions about Jesus, the church, and their own queerness. A common denominator among our newest attendees at Emmanuel Howard Park seemed to be their discomfort with the exclusion and judgment they felt they had experienced at other churches. Most of their questions seemed to be about questions of morality (judgment) and acceptance (hospitality).

I had an aversion to a social science approach to what I came to perceive as a theological question. That new people were arriving could mean anything. Whatever it might mean was not necessarily a testament to anything other than marketing or publicity or demographic shifts. The meaning of their arrival was a question to those already there. Was this evangelism? Was this the will of God or the result of our own efforts? Was Christ present in our own efforts? Yet it also seemed to me there was something in the stories I was hearing that spoke at theology or that spoke theologically. I agreed with the researcher Abraham Kaplan when he said, "If you can measure it, that ain't it!"[20] Yet research that was qualitative held out hope. An opportunity to listen closely (lovingly?) to the voices that were speaking to me might allow me to track the biblical story as it lived itself out in current lives. What did their stories have in common with the biblical story? What did our story as church have to do with the biblical story? We needed to listen to each other discerningly.

Bruce Berg described qualitative research as that which refers to the "meanings, concepts, definitions, characteristics, metaphors, symbols, and descriptions of things."[21] In Berg's presentation, research was never apart from theoretical analyses, but simply added another lens through which to view the subject matter. "Science" is defined as a specific and systematic way of, in part, understanding the impact of social realities on individuals.[22] That this impact is fluid and interactive, that individuals also affect social realities nuances the meaning of _objectivity_. Objectivity refers to the research's repeatability. Would the same subjects give the same or similar answers if asked by another researcher? I felt that those attending our church would.

The case study approach, because of the sensitivity of the questions I wanted to ask, and because of the limited number of individuals asked, seemed the most appropriate. A case study approach asks that the interviewer come to know the subject well, or well enough, to be able to speak with some degree of certainty about their motivations. It also assumes that what is true for one person may be generalizable. That even queers were, in some ways, predictable in their queerness was an assumption behind the questioning which occurred over several days in our sanctuary (a safe place indeed) and was recorded. That those who felt extremely marginalized had something important to say theologically to those who were not quite so marginalized or queer was another. What constituted "queer" was the first question I needed to ask theoretically.

Of course, the subjects were a small minority. Individuals who felt rejected by other churches or who had rejected other churches

20. Abraham Kaplan, _The Conduct of Inquiry_ (Scranton, Pa.: Chandler Publishing, 1998), 206.
21. Bruce L. Berg, _Qualitative Research Methods for the Social Sciences_ (Boston: Allyn and Bacon, 1998), 3.
22. Ibid., 11.

because of their own discomfort there might not represent a general-izable phenomenon, but that was not my interest anyway. My interest, which would take me back again and again to scripture, was, did this sense of rejection have anything to say about theology and evange-lism? Were these individuals messengers to our church, speaking in some way about our own Christian faith? Their voices interplayed with the voices of the New Testament in my own research.

Although I studied and included other theorists, two seminal the-orists, Judith Butler and Jacques Derrida, became most important in my thinking: Butler because of her work around the term "queer," and Derrida because of his investigation of the impossibility of true "gifting." If evangelism was a gift-giving process, whose gift was it? If the church had nothing to give, what was its role? How did Derrida's "economy of the circle"[23] inform as to both queerness and evange-lism? How did Butler's questioning of identity and identity politics speak to the lived stories of my congregants? How did they both aid in my queer reading of the strange heart of the New Testament? Both allowed a movement rather than a stasis to be considered an "answer" in research.

Biblically, I was being influenced by those like Raymond Brown who put questions to scripture about, for example, why certain dif-ferent varieties of church survived,[24] and those like Kathy Rudy and Eugene Rogers who asked ethical questions of scripture.[25] But more postmodern writers like Graham Ward, Catherine Keller, and Mark C. Taylor, for example, who blended Continental European theory with a fresh take on scripture, also left their mark on me.[26] What I found most exciting though was approaching scripture as though it might not make sense, as though it were more of a movement than a cohesion, as though its theme might be the lack of theme. Reading scripture queerly, I looked for the queerness (strangeness, undefinability) there.

---

23. Jacques Derrida, *Given Time, 1, Counterfeit Money* (Chicago: University of Chicago Press, 1992).

24. Raymond E. Brown, *The Churches the Apostles Left Behind* (New York: Paulist Press, 1984).

25. Kathy Rudy, *Sex and the Church* (Boston: Beacon, 1997); Eugene Rogers, *Sexuality and the Christian Body* (Oxford: Blackwell, 1999).

26. Graham Ward, *Barth, Derrida and the Language of Theology* (Cambridge: Cambridge University Press, 1995); Catherine Keller, *Apocalypse Now and Then* (Boston: Beacon, 1996); Mark C. Taylor, *Erring: A Postmodern A/Theology* (Chicago: University of Chicago Press, 1987).

Theologically, my influences were the orthodox to the neoorthodox to the postliberal to the poststructuralist, Barth to Rogers to Taylor, as examples. As I read widely I hoped to allow Christ to speak both from the pages of the books I read and in the voices of the congregants in our midst. Thus Del or Mary became conversational partners with theologians, theorists, and apostles.

Organizationally, this pan history, pan theory, conversation without answers only investigations, seemed to *be* queer (odd, difficult to decipher). Rather than try to regularize its ebb and flow too much, I elected to see it as a series of "beginnings again." To speak to Mary, for example, and then go back to the apostle John, to think about what church should be and then allow Kathy Rudy to speak on the subject of church as inclusive community so that the structure of the enquiry was an honest report on the process of the enquiry: this was how I proceeded. I hoped this was also biblical. As the synoptic gospels and John went back over the story of Jesus again and again, so the voices in this thesis went over and over the central theological questions leading to evangelism. In the same way, the economy of the circles described by Derrida would be mirrored in a circularity of process; interview, theoretical or theological discussion, scriptural input, interview. Rather than engaging one gospel, for example, and then applying a variety of questions to it, going back again and again with new questions seemed more relevant.

In adopting a style, I also wanted a text that would mirror all the different voices that seemed to speak to the issue at hand. Although Del and Mary, the transgendered/transsexuals, the queerest of the queer perhaps, provided the central raison d'être of the project, theirs were two of many tales. The tales told by theorists in a language more dense, less decipherable perhaps, needed to be honored. Sometimes "queerness" needs to be left to speak itself queerly (without overdefining).

I have tried to be understandable without losing the subtleties or the brilliance of the writings of Derrida, for example. Scripture too is full of new ways of using words and other ways of speaking. Again, I tried to be faithful to my influences. I tried to leave queerness alone as it spoke itself through all of the voices included without adding to its queerness (undecipherability). My failure to do so is perhaps part of the attempt itself. Again, the answer is that there are no answers (not even this one).

The Methodology in My History

The case study method of engaging the voices of our congregants was done with what I called a "continuum of queer" in mind. I chose individuals who seemed typically heterosexual, monogamous, and married at one end, to Mary, the transgendered person, and Del, queerly transsexual/gendered person at the other. I tried to include as much difference as I could within the continuum; men and women, small-town, big-city upbringing, for example. Since one of the operative questions was to discover why the queers (lesbigaytrans) interviewed had decided to come to our church (Emmanuel Howard Park) and in what way their queerness spoke to us about evangelism, my case group was self-defining except for the heterosexuals who were included as a sort of control.

How do the transgendered (possibly the queerest of the queer) in our society challenge the theory and practice of evangelism? This became the research question in the context of our congregation, Emmanuel Howard Park United, in inner-city Toronto, because they (the transgendered person) sought us out. The questions their presence put to me and us, combined as stated, with all the other questions around the issue of evangelism, are what form this study.

Kirby and McKenna's work highlighted the power relationship and its inequality in a research relationship that was also a professional relationship.[27] I share my own story as it shifts and changes and intersperses with the interviewees. The assent of the subjects of the interviews was even more important because it is merely a snapshot of an ongoing conversation. Creswell's discussion of the case study as part oral history works well, as oral history is the basis of scripture.[28] Myers's suggestion for corroboration in actual observations also fit well

27. S. Kirby and K. McKenna, *Experience, Research, Social Change: Methods from the Margins* (Toronto: Garamond Press, 1989).

28. J. Creswell, *Qualitative Inquiry and Research Design: Choosing among Five Traditions* (Thousand Oaks, Calif.: Sage Publications, 1998).

into a pastoral relationship since the individuals concerned were an active part of our church.[29]

The interviews were conducted with a tape recorder and after opening conversations regarding the topic. Subjects were told about my interest ahead of time, namely evangelism and the role of queers (lesbigaytrans) in our congregation, as well as the history of the United Church in this regard. All had participated in our "Introduction to Christianity" class and had some knowledge of our history, both theologically as the United Church and practically as Emmanuel Howard Park United Church. The questions were standardized although the interviews themselves were semistandardized. I wanted information, yet I wanted the information I received to take me where it wanted to go, rather than where I wanted to take it. We limited the interviews to two hours each, and all those interviewed expressed their interest in the topic. The interviews were an opportunity for them (some for the first time) to reflect theologically on their own lives. The analysis was a form of open coding, looking for themes that emerged, some expected and some not.

Since this study of the queer topic of the movement of evangelism and how it is lived in a congregation including the transgendered/transsexual persons is in a sense queer (done differently), theory is not corroborated or disproved by interviews. Rather, the interviews offer those interviewed an opportunity to look again at the scriptural imperative.

What does our story seem to say? What does the story of Jesus seem to say? What are the directional implications of the contradictions and similarities both within and between these stories?

Humility of outcome and process became part of the outcome and process. It was as if the interviews and experiences and voices of the writers studied opened up whole vistas, each of which would take a thesis of its own to investigate. If there was one assumption that seemed unshakeable in all of this research and the strange blends of beginnings again, it seemed to be the one that queers (those at the extreme margins of society and institutional church) did have

---

29. W. Myers, *Research in Ministry: A Primer for the Doctor of Ministry Program* (Chicago: Exploration Press, 1997).

something important to say that was both *from* and *to* Christian tradition.

As a method, qu(e)erying itself impressed me with its future both in the topics of theology and evangelism. Rather than looking for themes and concordances — the usual what, why, and how — I tried to listen to discrepancies, slippages, gaps, circularities, contradictions, what not, why not, and how not. Could the hermeneutic of suspicion that Ricoeur had bequeathed to theologians[30] be extended beyond its own boundaries? I suppose the bad news was that it was impossible to succeed with such a method. How would one measure success? I prayed that the good news was that it was impossible to fail.

---

30. Paul Ricoeur, *Freud and Philosophy: An Essay on Interpretation* (New Haven, Conn.: Yale University Press, 1970), 27.

Chapter Three

Qu(e)erying "Queer"

The First Beginning

If the term "queer" is to be a site of collective contestation, the point of departure for a set of historical reflections and futural imaginings, it will have to remain that which is, in the present, never fully owned, but always and only redeployed, twisted, queered from a prior usage and in the direction of urgent and expanding political purposes.[1]

Queer, long a term of derision for gays and lesbians, has been assumed as a rallying cry for a younger generation of gays, lesbians, and bisexuals. And the cry has not been so much for recognition as "just as good as" but perhaps for "more liberating than" straight alternatives. It is a cry that pushes the boundaries of identity politics and questions past politics. Yet it is a term that settles into itself as a gay or lesbian identity when confronted by homophobia but never far enough into itself as the prerogative of gays, lesbians, and bisexuals, however, so as to be entirely comfortable there.

"Queer" is an English word that continues to be used in an Oxford sense, unlike the almost always uniformly derogative — "nigger" for example. Queer Studies declare the legitimization of the term "queer" and yet the slippage of its meaning continues. As Butler also says:

> Indeed the term "queer" has been precisely the discursive rallying point for younger lesbians and gay men and, yet in other contexts, for bisexuals and straights for whom the term expresses an affiliation with anti-homophobic politics. That it can be such a discursive site whose uses are not fully constrained in advance ought to be safeguarded not only for the purposes of continuing to democratize queer politics, but also to expose, affirm and rework the specific historicity of the term.[2]

1. Judith Butler, *Bodies That Matter* (New York: Routledge, 1993), 228.
2. Ibid., 230.

Oddness, strangeness, weirdness, rareness, uniqueness, different-ness, queerness; these are or may be desirable. But is queerness possible? Is it possible to be different, which is to say, to make some sort of ontological break with ontology? Or is it a reiteration, a supplement, or predictably, a necessary "otherness" in a system of signification that demands an outside, a repressed? Is "queer" using the master's tools against the master, with the master orchestrating the usage all along? Just as heterosexuality needs homosexuality to define itself in a Fou-cauldian genealogy, does straightness need queerness? Is queer really so queer after all?

Also, is there a historicity to queer that can be reworked to rise to Butler's challenge, specifically a Christian historicity to the term that might claim Jesus Christ as the originary queer in Western thought — the originally hated Other, materially questionable, the undecidable around which a massive repression has constructed an ideology that eclipses the hole (which is Christ) with the whole that is heterosexual hegemony?

If the genealogy of Christianity has hidden the queerness of the one at its center, how has theology denied this Christ, or has it? How has theology, whether supportive of the full membership of lesbigay people in the body of Christ that is the church (which should there-fore include the opportunity to seek ordination) or not, denied the very queerness at its heart? If the margins are always queer, and the church should exist at the margins, why is the church so comfortably coexistent with monologic power?

Queerness as Break or Breakthrough

For Foucault, power relations define gender as a universal signifier and then cover up the construction.[3] Less apparent is the way in which power is subverted, if at all, and the a priori nature of Foucauldian power. Butler further radicalizes Foucault's position insofar as power works itself out on bodies by suggesting that bodies themselves are the effects of historical discourse and ideology. For Butler, inside/outside are also binary oppositions that are not originary and indeed neither

---

3. Michel Foucault, *The History of Sexuality*, vol. 2: *An Introduction*, trans. R. Hurley (New York: Pantheon, 1978).

is nature natural.[4] For her, sex is itself a construction; ground gives way to groundlessness.

Identity politics and identity itself is far from given. This is both its power and the possibility of subverting that same power. If the categories "woman" and "straight" are constructions, far from recovering some halcyon "originary woman" or "originary sexuality," boundaries become softened and change becomes possible. What has been constructed can be deconstructed.

To critics of deconstruction who think political action is impossible without foundationalism (the idealism and utopianism that masquerades sometimes as Christianity), Butler counters that only through the deconstruction of identity can new identities emerge. Derrida's endless supplementarity, endless *différance*, does not just endlessly repeat, but also produces agency and identity. The act of repetition is the very act of subjecthood. The labor of the subject is repetition, and the surplus value of repetition is the subject.[5]

This is rather like the old parlor game of whispering from one neighbor to another around a circle and finishing with a very different sentence than the one that began the chain. Each person out of their own collection of ideologies, subconscious language, historicities, contributes however unconsciously to the result. There is no originary at work, but there is supplementarity. Even the first phrase is *from* somewhere else.

Bert Archer and others speak from a poststructuralist perspective on the issue of sexual identity. He argues that "homosexuality," a construction with a particular date and place (1868, Germany by Karl Maria Kertbeny[6]) and "gay" are outmoded and inaccurate. Same-sex desire is and has been an aspect of human behavior for centuries, but the invention of the "homosexual" is historically specific and no longer descriptive of the way even queers live. He quotes many examples, among them Marcello D.:

---

4. Judith Butler, *Gender Trouble* (New York: Routledge, 1999).

5. Jacques Derrida, *Given Time*, 1, *Counterfeit Money* (Chicago: University of Chicago Press, 1992), 101.

6. Bert Archer, *The End of Gay and the Death of Heterosexuality* (Toronto: Doubleday, 1999), 67.

Homosexuality and heterosexuality don't exist. There doesn't exist an identity common to everyone. The homosexual model of life isn't a liberation. It is a limit to the personal experience of each of us. I'm not homosexual twenty-four hours out of twenty-four.... The risk today is living the ideology of life rather than the experience of life.[7]

Of course, Marcello is, one could say, living *another* ideology of life but still, it isn't quite gay and it is queer. Archer further examines the science behind sexual experience and finds that most humans are not exclusively gay or straight, in particular in the misquoted work of Kinsey.[8]

I first saw Archer interviewed in an apparently unlikely place, on the Michael Coran show. Michael Coran is a conservative Christian who was hoping in the person of Bert Archer to have found an ally in the church's war with gays and lesbians. After all, if we are never really purely gay or lesbian, then isn't it possible to *choose* to become something else?

This is exactly the scenario that those arguing a foundational basis for sexual orientation have feared. If homosexuality is not a "given," then homophobia can use this to argue for discrimination. If it is a lifestyle choice, then in light of a literalist reading of scripture, just say *no.* Where then does the *yes* to another of the same sex come from, if it does not come from our genes? Archer foresees this and argues, therefore, against the legitimization of heterosexuality as well. The *yes* to another (and this is where the problem comes) is made on the basis of *free* will.

Derrida began all of this in a sense, with deconstruction's refusal to "posit," its refusal to foreclose. Far from offering a critique of something, Derrida questions the shibboleths: forgiveness, gift giving, reason, originality — our favorite conceits. Where is the basis for ethical action, if we are simply the surplus value in an endless dance of supplementarity? Derrida might say in the very act of humility that sees us not as self-sustaining, directing identities but as caught in a web of great intricacy and possibility. Humility is the ethical call of the deconstructionist "I."

---

7. Ibid., 248.
8. Ibid., 145.

"Queer" is intuiting this, that the Enlightenment moorings of humanism are loose. The *cogito* of Descartes is decentered and fragmented. It is more flux than ground. Our boundaries are unstable, and our gaze is everywhere. "Queer" then is simply the person in the parlor whispering game who hears something no one else has heard to that point, or mishears, and slightly shifts the word — not enough so that we are no longer playing the game with the phrase, but enough so that new life is brought to an old game. In this way, one could claim the term and its chain of signification as potentially liberative. It is possibly, then, break and breakthrough of a possible outside of the circle, a birthplace of circling.

For Derrida and Butler, supplementarity is as close to freedom as we get, and faith is engaging in its economy with gusto. Life is an endless exegesis.

> *Know* still what giving *wants to say, know how to give,* know what you want and want to say when you give, know what you intend to give, know how the gift annuls itself, commit yourself even if commitment is the destruction of the gift by the gift, give economy its chance.[9]

A messianism without a Messiah, a creation without Creator except in the *excess* which is produced in movement. The fall, for Derrida, is real, even as the place from which we have fallen is unknowable. Ontology, maybe, but ontologists, never.

We are left, in Derrida, with a testimony a priori:

> For one will never, it is impossible and it must not be done, reconcile the value of a testimony with that of knowledge or of certitude. One will never, it is impossible and it must not be done, reduce the one to the other.[10]

A Christian could draw no better picture of sin, of life after the Fall than that. For Barth as well, endless exegesis is the call to the creature. The best that we do is mirror dimly the acts of Jesus Christ, and yet here also is a sort of freedom found. The significant difference is that for Christians there is a Messiah and for Christians there is a Creator.

---

9. Derrida, *Given Time*, 30.
10. Jacques Derrida, *Passions* (Paris: Galilee, 1993), 70–71.

There is a *who* responsible for the circle of whisperers, yet along with Derrida, we provide, at best, a proximate witness. "Jesus is Lord" would be better written, "(Jesus is Lord?)."

Free will, in Archer's sense, is an impossibility for both. In both Derrida and Barth a call has been issued, a prior claim upon us. That call, whether from Christ or not, is the place of the ethical.

Qu(e)erying might also be the place of a political defense of lesbigays. It is no longer that one cannot love another of the opposite sex (assuming the sexual dichotomy), but that one loves one of the same sex despite all the incentives to the contrary. It is no longer that we love another of the same sex because we *choose* to but because the Other (God) has chosen to claim us in this way. When we speak of covenantal union, whether legal or not, we speak of a union brought about by God. The margins of queerness, the margins where queers find themselves in relation to the church triumphant rather than the church martyred, is, we need to prove, exactly where the church discovers its own Christ. Where they are welcomed, whether sexually queer or any other sort of queer, is the place from where the call addresses the church.

This then demands that the Christian defense of brothers and sisters who choose to love those of the same sex be grounded not in pseudo-science or liberal apologetics but in scripture and theology. These, I argue later, work very effectively in contesting what passes as Christian "morality."

The other argument, again from scripture, is that queerness is scriptural. Jesus Christ can be claimed as queer not because of so-called historical evidence, as all historical evidence being in part a mirror of the historian is simply a different sort of construction, but because of scriptural imperative. An unknowing precedes and makes historical research possible. History as presented, history as passed on is predicated on never really knowing what actually occurred. This then is also a possible point of reconciling Christians. Jesus is queer, this I know, for the Bible tells me so.

As children, strange (queer) children, how would we read Jesus? In what way can we make the claim that Jesus was and is, since we claim him as alive, queer?

Our Queer Lord (b)

What are Christians anyway? Even the term itself implies a surety of sorts. Are Christians defined as those who claim "Jesus is lord" even though they never really comprehend what that means? Are Christians defined by claiming they are Christian whether or not they would say "Jesus is lord"? Christians are here defined as those who pray to be Christian, not quite knowing what that may look like. Christians are here defined as those who follow the call of Christ in the world.

When claiming our own originary (sort of), our own *outside* or our own margins, the danger lurks of conflating the psychotic, or the fall from meaning, with the birthplace of meaning or the originary queer. This is the safeguard of the text of proximate witness, or the canon of scripture, and yet perhaps we have been too careful in domesticating scripture. Perhaps scripture also *bleeds* like Christ, and in its very heterogeneity calls the faithful to let the wounds alone. So perhaps the question to begin with when we look at scripture is: what does that call sound like?

Mark

In Mark's gospel, Jesus enters from the margins, from nowhere, from Nazareth. He has no personal history, no personal historicity. Yet he is somehow all of Israel. He arrives, is baptized, and immediately the movement of the text is hurried as though there is little time left until the end of his ministry (1:9–11). He becomes a vortex of activity, catching humans, who in turn will be catchers of humans (1:16–19). He teaches, drawing people in and casting demons out, and raises people up (1:21–31). We are not told the content of his teaching or the content of his message, only that "people came to to him from all quarters" (Mark 1:45). He is in some strange way the content of his own teaching.

Jesus is the center of activity, but the center lacks substance. It is ephemeral, nonspecific, undecidable. He warns sternly about not telling anybody about his work, and people immediately break his trust by proclaiming it far and wide (1:40–45). He forgives sins blasphemously, according to Pharisaic law, and eats with social outcasts, never leaving the margins, always on the edges of temple life. He announces, "Those who are well have no need of a physician but those who are sick. I have come to call not the righteous but sinners" (Mark 2:17).

Immediately, he is shown to be a religious lawbreaker, especially where laws of propriety are concerned. Jesus eats and drinks during fasts, works on the Sabbath, heals on the Sabbath, and declares himself Lord over the Sabbath (2:18–28). He turns from his biological family and declares the sinners and misfits that he attracts around him to be his true family (3:33–35). Jesus teaches in parables, metaphors that immediately are supplemented and misunderstood, immediately dispersed. Only privately does he divulge secrets. The secrets themselves, the hermeneutic, are never divulged.

In Mark's fourth chapter, Jesus begins to show his primacy over the elements of nature. He is *prior to materiality*, as Butler might say (4:35–41). He is also prior to the life/death binary, long before his own resurrection, for he raises Jairus's daughter (5:39–42). Interestingly, he is only without power where he is best known, in his own hometown. There he can do no miracles for there they *knew him* (Mark 6:5).

Jesus sends forth the twelve with strict instruction to continue moving, to take little, to remain in flux (6:7–13). His feeding of the five thousand *is* dissemination, a very symbol of symbolism, a metaphor of metaphoricity (6:37–44). Of course he walks on water (6:48–52). We are part of the secret, yet not. We are hearing what we are forbidden, by Jesus himself, at every turn, to hear. But are we? The author who casts himself as eyewitness is privy perhaps to a secret that we are not. Jesus tells the twelve and us, who listen in, about his death and resurrection.

Those that witness his miracles are forbidden to speak. They do not obey him. Interestingly, it is in disobedience that obedience is born. Had they (disciples, others) been obedient, we would not hear of their obedience or disobedience to Jesus.

The gift of Jesus is outside the economy of the whispering circle. He whispers to his disciples in our hearing; to learn what is whispered one must die. We are called to faith and repentance for lack of faith. His call, already supplemented and disseminated, is like his body and

blood, passed out over and over. We are called to faith in the dissemination, which is the proclamation of the Word, in the author(s) of
the scripture, the eyewitness, the whisper half heard, misheard, overheard. We are warned in chapter 13 that there will be false prophets
who will mislead us, that the end of the circle will come in apocalypse,
that the end of dissemination will be like its beginning, only known
by the Father, a secret, even to Jesus. Keep awake. But for what, to
what? How do we know false from true? How do we know — Derrida
would ask — counterfeit from real currency, "real" currency being the
agreed-upon deception?

Jesus remains silent before us, before Pilate (15:5). We must believe
the belief of the believers — believers who at every turn betray him,
even the eyewitnesses like Peter and Judas. The women believe, the
women who from the far edges of the margins of patriarchy are the
only ones left at the foot of the cross and the first witnesses of the
resurrection (16:9–13). Peter, upon whom the church was built, must
learn it from them. What does Peter learn? Peter learns that there is
an empty tomb.

Christ does appear but in different forms and meeting disbelief.
He dies, the worst of evangelists if evangelism is church growth, for
almost all his followers have abandoned him. Finally the eleven are
convinced but clearly faith is still to be tested and this faith in faith,
like the flux of the water of baptism, must be repoured and repoured.
Faith must be, in a sense, found wanting, just short of faith, to be
reaffirmed as faith. It is never certainty. It is never fast. That is why
it is always and ever faith. Its movement is from the margins, in to
the decentered center which is Christ (X), and out to the margins
again. This is the inception of the circularity of Christian being, the
whispering circle.

John

> The wind blows where it chooses; you hear the sound of it, but you do
> not know where it comes from or where it goes. So it is with everyone
> who is born of the Spirit. (John 3:8)

Jesus as the light of the world is the Word incarnate in human form
but it is no word in particular. Rather, the Word is he who is the Word.

And this Word flouts laws, especially purity laws, this timeless/timed man who is still man as well as more than a man. This man who is both Jew and redefines Jew. This Jesus who is bread from heaven and yet never eaten up, has blood that is to be drunk, yet always available. Jesus who calls the twelve including the one who will betray him (this devil he does not cast out).

The crowd, of course, thinks Jesus is the devil, possessed. He is certainly not of this world. But of what world is he? He is sent by someone from whom he is never, in a sense, separate. There is an undecidability, a rift in the very core of this God. He announces that he is here to restore sight to the blind but also to make the seeing blind (9:39)! Those that claim to see are judged guilty. The faithful will know him by his voice alone, not the content but the sound; the content doesn't seem important (e.g., 10:4, 16).

John's Jesus both points away from himself to the Father but also to himself as one with the Father, both to the one who sent him and to himself as the Ontological One. He is both/and. He is both the originary and points to a more prior originary. In this way, he claims originary as Derrida would understand it. But unlike Derrida, he claims it originarily. He is strange, odd, weird, unusual, unique; queer. John's Jesus turns the tables.

Jesus chooses the disciples and us through them, through him, through the power of the Holy Spirit, to the Godhead which is, in a sense, also Jesus. He intimates again that there is more he could say, a secret he could divulge but doesn't, even to the disciples, but that the Holy Spirit will speak with authority, the Holy Spirit which is and is not distinct from Jesus, who we will and will not see again. Figures of speech will be replaced with plain words, but not now. Now, Jesus responds to Pilate that his kingdom is not of this world, it is *elsewhere. His work is to bear witness to the truth as was John's to bear witness to him. It is always elsewhere.* It is not Jesus but Pilate who asks, "What is truth?" (John 18:38). There is no question that for Jesus there is truth; it is what he points to, it is what he is. But it is nothing to be said; again, as in Mark, Jesus is silent.

Even Jesus' garments are dispersed, and his mother is bequeathed as mother to a disciple. The risen Christ is recognized by wounds, marks, in the catching of fish (people). They recognize him but aren't sure.

His sayings are also fading like his person. The disciple, John writes, whom Jesus loved (which one is that?) is thought to be promised eternal life but this was a mishearing. The "disciple whom Jesus loved" is the real witness to the proximate witness who was John the writer (or was it John that Jesus loved?). Is the author the narrator because we know that his testimony was true (John 21:24)? Does this mean that the author's testimony is suspect? But then again there is so much more, John tells us, that he tells us he won't tell us (John 21:25).

Luke

Jesus is the one who lives an existence of divine temporality and wills to live an instance of human temporality. There is no room for him who is born on the road, but it is announced by angels to the lowly shepherds and Jesus is named by angels (2:1–20). He is recognized as Messiah by an old man and an old woman, Anna and Simeon (2:25–36) and soon amazes learned men with his knowledge claiming his house as a temple (2:41–49). But what he said and why it amazed anyone is unknown, and even his own parents did not understand him (2:50).

Luke gives Jesus' genealogy back to Adam and through Adam to God (3:21–38). It is a genealogy of the circle, God begins and ends it. He is tempted by a scripture-quoting Satan who in doing so uses scripture against scripture, in scripture (4:1–13). The devil misunderstands that he is speaking to the one who proclaims scripture and is the content of scripture. Luke understands that this is a sort of wound *in* scripture that Luke must attempt to remedy. For Jesus breaks the law, fulfills the law, and is the law. Jesus *is* the words from Isaiah that he reads in synagogue (4:16–20).

Jesus preaches the subversion of all binaries and calls for the impossible in the Sermon on the Mount (6:20–38). If we are dealt what we deal out, we are doomed, but we interpret it as words of love and salvation (or does Luke?). A woman of ill repute is praised, and Simon, a disciple, is admonished (7:36–48).

Luke's Jesus is itinerant, always moving, homeless everywhere. The disciples proliferate, disseminate, all of them miracle workers (9:1–6). Crowds push in and around him to listen to his stories, told within the story. Always the kingdom is preached, a seed, yeast, supplementarity itself. Metaphor after metaphor accumulates. They confuse and make clear.

The disciples are, like supplementarity itself, more of the same but different. They are to be treated as if like Jesus himself, yet are not Jesus himself.

We are told in the story of the Good Samaritan that our neighbors are not who we think they might be (10:30–36), that the best way to teach is to tell stories that may or may not mean what we think they mean (parables), and that a sign of wickedness is to ask for a sure sign rather than have faith (11:29). He admonishes the Pharisees for making an exhibition of their faith and not having a hidden, interior faith (11:37–41), the lawyers for burdening the public with law and not engaging with their singularity, their otherness we might say (11:45–52).

Luke's Jesus is not afraid to contradict himself in the space of a few lines. He says if the reader/listener/disciple/we disown him we will be disowned and then immediately says we may speak words against him and be forgiven (12:8–10). In the midst of contradiction and the chaos of crowds he warns against anxiety and speaks of storing up treasures in heaven (12:27–40). We are not surprised, we who are not sure if "we" are the ones addressed, to hear that Jesus' mission is to bring dissension (12:52–53).

There is never a straight answer given to a question. There are stories, as the Lucan narrative is a story of stories. We are told by Jesus to hate what is most familiar, especially family (14:26) and yet to gather in those who have been lost (15:4). Finally we have a parable that rewards the one who is lost, before he repents, "But, while he was still a long way off" (Luke 15:20), the repentance at that point being a secret between the listeners listening in on the listeners and Jesus himself. This is a very different sort of justice: one that rewards dishonest stewards (16:1–8), one that makes all the demands of the law but forgives those that break it more than the one that leads them astray (16:16–17:2). An apocalyptic tenor to Jesus' words suggests that justice is not of this world but of some other, and yet it is the same Jesus who states, "The kingdom of God is among you!" (Luke 17:21).

Always, this Jesus calls to those from the margins and calls for dissemination. Parables proliferate even as the content within the parable concerns itself with dissemination (19:11–27).

No authority is claimed for his words (20:8). The apocalypse will happen at the end of time, but the end of time is their lifetime (and ours, listeners of listeners) (21:32). Interestingly at the Last Supper, the listeners who are listening are also privy to a secret even the disciples do not know: who is to betray Jesus and that they, all around the table, will in some way betray him; that, even Luke does not fully realize. The text speaks against its author but not, one has faith, against its Author.

Jesus references another more primary source. *Différance* is then, closer to Christ than *différance* (Derrida) would like to say.[11] Jesus looks back at scripture, above to the Father (e.g., 22:37, 42). Although he is, if anyone ever is, at the center of the circle, there is yet a more primary origin, a more truthful truth. There is a more originary origin.

As Luke ends, we are left with disciples who still do not recognize Jesus as Messiah, who do not recognize Jesus as alive. We are left with Jesus speaking of himself in the third person, speaking to us, who are mystified through the writings of those mysterious to us. We are left with the trace of what once was, through the whispering centuries-old circle (24:26–48).

Matthew

Jesus announces early in Matthew that he is a supplement/fulfillment of the Torah (5:17). He is also an inversion of the Torah, for he is the saved child, as Israel was the saved nation (2:16). He is Jewish and judgmental of the Jewish, calling the Sadducees and Pharisees vipers (3:7). It is Israel that needs healing, the margins teach the center (10:5–8).

We are not to judge others, and it is not enough to say we believe, to say we have faith, but we must do the will of the Father (7:21). Everything will be made clear by the One who knows everything, but

---

11. *Différance*: I would refer the reader to Caputo's discussion of the many meanings of Derrida's *différance* in John Caputo, *Radical Hermeneutics* (Bloomington: Indiana University Press, 1987), 129–273.

it is not clear, at least not to the disciples and the listeners around the circle (8:27). What is clear is that Jesus has come to bring the sword and not peace, to both those who receive him and those who don't (10:34, 40). Reward is always deferred. The ones called are tired and simple, the ones promised the sword and rest at the same time (11:28).

Jesus tells his disciples that he speaks in parables to "them." But are we not "them"? Or are we disciples (them)? He does not tell the disciples anything but parables. He tells them that they "see" and "hear" and yet they don't really know what they see and hear, or at least they are not faithful enough, ever. The parables he continues to tell them are about sowing and yeast, parables of growth and dissemination, but of what? He utters secrets in the form of yet other secrets, metaphors of other metaphors (13:18–50). The kingdom of Heaven is *like*, it *is* not anything. The disciples nod their heads and say they understand. But we (the disciples) wonder. Even Jesus does not fully understand, because an unknown woman corrects his knowledge (15:25–28). Peter, the rock, who says he knows Jesus to be the Messiah, sells him out.

The disciples learn it is practically impossible to be saved by their own work (19:25) and yet impossible to be saved without it (25:35–40). Justice is delivered by God and not humans, and humans will never have a clear idea of why or of the basis of justice (20:14–16). In a kingdom, the kingdom of Jesus, binaries are upset, masters serve, the marginalized teach, and a woman instructs God — a God who is a Jewish peasant. Faith will provide everything, but it is not the faith of the disciples (or ours), which is ever and always shown to be wanting, and yet everything will be provided for us. Good and bad alike are invited to the banquet, but only the chosen get to remain and only the king knows who is chosen (22:10–14).

Everything hangs on "Love the Lord your God with all your heart, with all your soul, and with all your mind. Love your neighbor as yourself" (Matt. 22:37–39). And indeed that is all that one can do, to be sure that is, of crucifixion. Yet there is more than death promised; there is life but only after death, a life we will never know. A life that is whispered, a secret that is never divulged, a promise that is never kept within knowledge. A life that is never bounded by knowledge, never foreclosed, never known. We come as close as wine is to blood and as flesh to bread, as close as symbols of metaphors, both in us (as drunk) and on us (as our hands) whispered down through the centuries.

Matthew's Jesus will fulfill scripture. A Jesus who can and could at any moment evade death chooses to go to death against his own choice (Matt. 26:42).

A Jesus who is one with the Father calls out to the Father. The wounded Jesus calls out through the ink of a wounded text. There is slippage at the heart of the one we call God; our God is pierced, wounded. *What God has rent asunder, no human can put back together.*

Our Queer Lord (b)

But what of the other meaning of "queer," as in not heterosexual? Jesus Christ may represent a break in God as ontological truth, a God both human and divine that qu(e)eries everything we thought we knew about a removed, omnipotent master of the universe. In Derridean terms, Jesus Christ may represent a break in the economy of the circle or a birthplace of the economy. Jesus Christ may represent a God of *différance*.[12] Jesus Christ may be the call from the whirlwind, a call against God as ontology or ontologies, a call to love as faith, as giving the economy of the gift its chance, as Derrida might put it. But is/was he queer sexually?

To raise the question is not to raise the question of Jesus' possible homosexuality. It is not another attempt to legitimate homosexuality. It is a pointed attempt to delegitimate heterosexuality, to subvert hetero-normativity right at the inception, right where the defenders of hetero-normativity would have it begin: in scripture. Did Jesus Christ espouse or demonstrate a queer sexuality?

In engaging the question, postpoststructuralists would hope to parenthesize the word "sexuality" and examine it transhistorically in the manner of Foucault. It may, in other words, have nothing to do with

---

12. For our purposes here, *différance* is the work of the economy of the circle, always failing to set out to do what it intends, achieving something slightly different instead. This break in God is represented by the work of the Son, not God creator or Father, and after/with Jesus the existence of the paraclete.

genitals. It may have to do with anything invested with libidinal energy in a Freudian sense, or desire itself. Or to paraphrase, following Jorge Luis Borges:

There were many sexualities in the kingdom,

a. Those who preferred partners to look like fishermen.

b. Those who did not want partners.

c. Those who were excited by eating and drinking.

d. Those who liked to pray in public so that others could see them.[13]

Perhaps where theologians make a mistake is to assume a nineteenth- and twentieth-century understanding of identity as ontological. This is a historical, philosophical, and theological blunder, for biblically we are called to have faith only in God. The foundational error, if you will, of foundationalism in the area of sexuality is that it affects our reading of scripture when the reverse should be the warrant. If "male" and "female" are not categories of identity but of performativity, what might it mean that they are the creation of God, or that Jesus Christ was male?

The gospels do, however, tell us that Jesus Christ called his followers *away* from their families and claimed that those who did not hate their families could not follow him. He claimed the preeminence of faith-based communities over any sort of other living arrangement. There are no hints of couplings among the disciples. He breaks purity laws consistently and often.

In addition women and those who break purity laws are the ones he prefers to associate with. He calls and is called by the Other. He calls and is called upon by others.

Jesus Christ, as attested to by scripture, is antimoral where morality has to do with creaturely forms of conduct, with distinctions of rightness and wrongness. Under his standard of ethical conduct we are all judged wrong (and forgiven). We are pointed to love of God and neighbor. Hence the "call" from God (as the disciples were called) is the ethical direction. Since Jesus Christ is alive, Christians contest, his call is present to us. We are called to discern that call's nature in the moment.

---

13. Jorge Luis Borges, *Ficciones* (New York: Grove Press, 1962).

I could be with a man or woman. I have always known that. But I met Sara and she loved me and stood by me when others abandoned me and in the depths of my depression, even when I was suicidal. I fell in love with her, and I feel ours is a covenantal relationship. It would be wrong to leave her just so that I could be in a "typical" marriage. To hurt her, to abandon her; that didn't ever seem Christian. I love her with all of my being, and whether the church recognizes my love for her and her love for me, God does.[14]

Does it matter what the speaker's genitals are? Or, as Christian, is the more important question not whether she or he responds to the call of Christ?

If sexuality and gender are "performative" rather than ontological, Jesus performed as queerly as one can imagine, given the reactions of the powers of his day. Kathy Ruby in her book *Sex and the Church* gives an example of the discernment process, postresurrection:

The central question of contemporary Christian politics today should not be "Should homosexuals be ordained?" or "Should homosexuals be allowed to marry?" but rather, "What does any collection of sexual practices have to do with the Christian life? How does having sex affect one's relationship with God and with the Christian community?"[15]

Of course, our "neighbor" extends beyond the Christian community, and the call may very well be, in the moment, the ordination or marriage of those involved in same-sex unions (or not).

Eugene F. Rogers Jr. makes such a move when he discusses the trinity and love:

Christians must norm their use of the word "love" by the love by which Jesus pleases the Father. The love by which Jesus pleases the Father is a love that pleases him already in the Trinitarian life, and by which human beings see directed toward them in the *philanthropia*, a love which the Scriptures describe as erotic.[16]

Yet, he ends with a moral call for "homosexuals" to marry and the church to recognize their marriages, which is not the New Testament call but the churches' or the theologians'.

---

14. "B.," Conversation with author, February 2000.
15. Kathy Rudy, *Sex and the Church* (Boston: Beacon, 1997), 207.
16. Eugene F. Rogers Jr., *Sexuality and the Christian Body* (Oxford: Blackwell, 1999), 222.

That Jesus Christ had a penis is probably as close to factual as anything historical, but the meaning of his body, the meaning of "maleness" to his identity, is not. He was the very definition of human-ness, he was the true human, Scripture does tell us. In being the true human and truly Divine, in being the queer beginning of queer-ness, in making any ontological claims about humanness, Jesus Christ's maleness is a mystery not tritely solved by twentieth or twenty-first centurions. That God created us male and female is an invitation to discover the mysteries and freedoms in that revelation. Nothing in Genesis, one might argue, states that the male and female created was linked to a certain set of genitalia.

Leo Steinberg makes an excellent case for the very sexual Jesus Christ in terms of his penis in *The Sexuality of Christ in Renaissance Art and in Modern Oblivion*.[17] Renaissance artists saw Christ with erections, both in infancy and adulthood. They had no "moral" qualms about his active sexuality. Dutifully, post-Renaissance artists painted over the more shocking examples. In terms of a genealogy of morals, sex and Christ as understood through artistic depictions has changed as much as an understanding of "acceptable sexual expression."

More important for the Christian are Paul's words in Galatians: "There is no longer Jew or Greek, there is no longer slave or free, male or female; for all of you are one person in Christ Jesus" (Gal. 3:28). Or, Jesus Christ is both Jew and Greek, *male and female*, slave and free. It is the very definition of queer.

"Systematics" is an almost violent term when applied to the Jesus of scripture. He was most unsystematic. He was the very breaking of all systems: systems of thought, systems of identity, systems of power, sys-tems of religion. He was silent, we recall, to the statement or question, "What is truth?" (John 18:28). He is dogmatic in his antidogmatism. Pastoral, moral, almost any term that might further demarcate theolo-gies from each other, seem problematic when we as witnesses appeal to the gospels' proximate witness. As we read through the Word, back to Genesis and forward (back/around) to Revelation, the wounds, the slippage is not covered or healed but rather grows. Jesus Christ is most

---

17. Leo Steinberg, *The Sexuality of Christ in Renaissance Art and in Modern Oblivion* (Chicago: University of Chicago Press, 1996).

certainly a discursive site whose use (for us) is never fully constrained in advance (to paraphrase Butler).[18]

The questions that arise are rather, like Heidegger's task with philosophy, to go back to the beginning of the process of enquiry and ask the questions again: qu(e)erying from the whispering circle still perhaps, but for the hard of hearing, the simple, the sinful, the ones scripture tells us Jesus liked to eat with. "Queer" is a beginning.

> In the end, full inclusion may mean that neither homosexuality nor the heterosexual norm will be left intact. Indeed there may be no Christianity for queers, although there may be a queer Jesus.[19]

The prayer perhaps is that what is left is a queer Christianity, as queer as Jesus. The prayer perhaps is that Christianity becomes a little less comfortable.

Beginning with Evangelos

I have no idea why queer messengers began to arrive at Emmanuel Howard Park United Church. It started to occur before we gained notoriety for performing the first legalized same-sex wedding. We held a free community dinner, but so did many other churches. We preached inclusion, but so did others.

The change and the gift, the whispers that changed the meanings of evangelism for us, began undoubtedly with Del, for Del was the queerest of the queer and seemed prophetic in her witness from the beginning. This work is in many ways a testament to her.

---

18. Judith Butler, *Bodies That Matter* (New York: Routledge, 1993).

19. Laurel C. Schneider, "Homosexuality, Queer Theory, and Christian Theology," *Religious Studies Review* 26 (January 2000): 3.

Chapter Four

A Girl Like Him — Del

Beginning the Interviews

Our evening services started about six months into my ministry. Our church is situated downtown on the edge of one of the poorest areas of the inner city. Once, the area had been different. Once, two services saw over a thousand people worshiping on a Sunday. When I arrived, we would be lucky to see fifty at one service. The morning service grew to around a hundred-plus in the five years that I had ministered there and the evening service from zero to around thirty to forty. On high holy days like Easter and Christmas, both would double in size. Increasingly the morning service attracted young twenty- and thirty-somethings with families. The evening service, however, with its free community supper was almost exclusively composed of low-income and marginalized people.

At first in the evening, we ate and then had worship. The evening congregants who composed our newly formed "Outreach Committee" voted to change the order and worship first. Many women did not like to stay too late, and this allowed them and others to worship and eat. Many simply felt that worship was as important as eating. At first we did not take an offering as our evening congregants were among the poorest in the city. The Outreach Committee voted to have an offering. Our dinner and worship started as two people, myself and a helper. It gradually swelled to eight to ten and then to its present thirty to forty. Evening congregants joined in a number of other activities around the church, including becoming members and sitting on various committees.

Del[1] first walked into our community supper and sat alone, eating. The evening service took place before the dinner at that time, and

---

1. "Del" is a pseudonym.

almost all participants joined us for the service and stayed for dinner. Del was one of the few who carefully avoided anything to do with church and never entered the sanctuary, even to see if the service was over. Many months passed, and although I tried to introduce myself to her, there was never any ensuing small talk. In fact, Del preferred not to talk to anybody.

Del is about six feet tall, average weight, thirty or forty, long gray-black hair, glasses, native looking. She always wore jeans and a T-shirt. A time or two, I would find her playing the piano in the room where we ate. She was obviously a skilled and able jazz/blues keyboard player. I commented on how beautifully she played.

After a number of months, she ventured into the sanctuary and sat off to one side in the transepts, observing. Gradually she sat in the main body of the church and even began to sing and participate. One evening she decided I was safe enough to speak to. We began to have small conversations about our lives and about music. Del even played hymns for me one night when our regular music director was absent.

During one of our conversations I explained to Del my phobia about playing. I told her that having been trained as a classical violinist at an early age and having been on scholarship, I found the expectations to practice and perform excruciating. I told her that at one time, to avoid a lesson, I had even poured boiling water on my hands. This story became a recurrent theme with Del as she attempted to explicate her own life. She began to tell me of her childhood, how her father would beat her if she did not practice the piano.

One day she arrived early for service and asked if she could speak to me alone. We found a quiet space where Del told me more of her story. She trusted me enough. Following is a verbatim of parts of that conversation.

Del: I want to tell you something because I think you can handle it.

Cheri: Go ahead.

Del: I've listened to your sermons, and more to the point I've watched the way you are with people here, even people who are just taking advantage of your generosity. So I've decided that you can handle this. I want you to know about me. I've told you about my fucked-up childhood and I've told you about the music stuff, why I don't play unless I'm really moved to play. But what I haven't told you is that I'm transgendered. You see, I'm not a man, I'm a woman. It's something I've always known about myself. It's a spiritual and sexual path. Can you handle that?

Cheri: Of course. (I shared with her some of my interest in queerness for this project.) Have you had surgery?

Del: I'm taking hormones and I went to a clinic in Vancouver, but I don't need to go the whole surgical route. I'm not interested in the whole gay liberation thing. They're just the same old shit. I wrote an article about getting thrown out of a dyke bar because they said I was a man. Trannies are universally hated. I've been suicidal most of my life. I'm on 60mg of Prozac now, and it doesn't even make a dent. Man, I've been so low for so long. And Vancouver was just part of the problem. I was "killed" there, stabbed and left for dead. I had a near-death experience, figured I have some sort of reason to be alive. I've had girlfriends. I've been well socialized, you know. I can do all of the "male" thing if I have to. Have you seen the movie, *Boys Don't Cry?*

Cheri: No. Sorry.

Del: It says it all about being a trannie. I was bummed out for weeks after that one. But the director really nailed it, and I don't usually like that Hollywood crap. Go see it.[2]

I did. I also spent many hours speaking and prayerfully engaging with the queer that is/was Del. Several aspects "called" me. First and foremost, the "man" I saw before me was not at all feminine in any way. She was very male in all the ways that we are used to "seeing" men. Interestingly, Del was also not Native. She was Eastern European by descent. She was living a marginal existence, on welfare because of her bipolar disorder and with a history of drug and alcohol abuse, yet sophisticated, articulate. There was no way she had of knowing that my interest outside of church had anything to do with "queerness," yet she had outed herself to me. Not male, not female. Certainly it was true, not native/originary in any way. Another conversation:

Del: I read a review about *Boys Don't Cry* written by a dyke. She said the usual bullshit that the principal character was just a lesbian who couldn't handle her "true" nature. This is the same old bullshit I

---

2. Conversation with author, October 2, 2000.

always get from gays and lesbians. The doctor at the Gender Clinic in Vancouver after years still didn't have a clue. She asked me, "What is a woman anyway?"

Cheri: One of the "women"[3] I'm reading suggests that our sex is not essential but performative. We are what we do?

Del: What does a woman do? (*Laughs*)

Cheri: Beats me. (*Laughter*) Maybe it has more to do with being marginalized. Maybe a "woman" is the one who is marginalized. Whoever is marginalized is a woman? That's one of the reasons I like the term "queer."

Del: Yeah. I like "queer" too. I've always considered myself queer.

Cheri: What do you think about power being the main issue, rather than sexuality?

Del: Both maybe. Being a woman is definitely a spiritual path.

Cheri: You don't mind me using this conversation and the others we have, do you?

Del: It's just a conversation. I'll forget about it as soon as I leave tonight. I have lots of conversations. Most of what everyone tells me is bullshit. I have so many conversations in the course of a day. Use anything you want.

Del had successfully kicked drugs, heroin and cocaine. She had that old hippies' disdain for cops and authority, institutions and order. She related to me because she saw some sort of common thread, because she, on some level, believed me. She liked the role I saw in her of prophet. It resonated with some sort of role she saw in herself as prophet or, she would more likely say, shaman, in the sense of "teacher." Although Del was too humble to ever offer this, her face lit up when we spoke of it. Del liked Carlos Castaneda books. She liked Miles Davis. And she played beautifully — although to play was as painful for her as finding the way through the world, a world she considered hell at times. A world that for her was hell at times.

Del: In Native cultures, transsexual and transgendered persons were considered Shamans. In our culture we're loathed. Every trannie I know is suicidal.

---

3. Judith Butler.

Cheri: Have you checked out any support groups?

Del: Nah. They're the most depressing things I've ever seen. A bunch of suicidal trannies sitting around depressing each other. I don't need that.

Del really was/is queer. It struck me that even if most of everything she said was suspect, it was still undeniably queer. As research, as a case study, even the skeptical researcher had to admit that the *form* the fantasy took, if it was/is a fantasy, was still queer. Why claim fraudulently that you are a woman? Why claim fraudulently that you are a transgender person? Even if counterfeit, the claim itself was marginal, the claiming was marginal, was queer, was transgressive. Could there, is there, any such thing as a *real* transgender person? Is there such a thing as a real counterfeit? Or what is a *real* woman or man? Aren't we, all of us, counterfeit in some way? Aren't we, all of us, trying to be female or male? Again, operatively speaking, Del performed as both. Del saw herself as both. Del was both. Her non-Christianity was as transgressive as her gender. She prayed against prayer. One night she attended a small group Reiki[4] session that we hold weekly in our church. We always close with prayer. Del prayed:

> I don't believe in God but I'd like to pray. I'd like to pray for all the women who were burned and tortured as witches in the Middle Ages and all the queers who the church has persecuted and who are still persecuted.

I thought it sounded like a prayer for there to be a God, a prayer for a God who might answer prayer. It was also a way of asking a question of me. How could I reconcile my part in a church that persecuted queers and women when we (the United Church) were supposedly welcoming to women and queers? We talked more. Del continued to come to worship, to sing hymns, to argue, speak, question about God. I continued to converse with Del about all matters queer, to worship, sing hymns, argue, speak, question whether she represented a call from God. One night we argued about music.

Cheri: As a classically trained musician I found it difficult to hear Delta blues. I simply heard it as "simple." Then I learned to love it, and it

---

4. Reiki is a hands-on healing and meditative practice.

was a quantum shift in my consciousness. Similarly I learned to really love some forms of hip-hop, like the Beastie Boys.

Del: The Beastie Boys are crap!

Cheri: What do you mean?

Del: I mean they're crap. And everything you said about complex and simple is crap. Good Delta blues is far more complex than Beethoven.

Cheri: Well, what I meant was in the usual meaning of the words.

Del: That's what I mean too. There's more complexity in the blues. The rest is brainwashing. Remember the boiling water on your hands.

I remembered.

One night, Del showed me her wounds from the stabbing incident in Vancouver. She rolled up her shirt and pointed out to me where each knife thrust had entered. She needed me to know how real that experience had been. There was a wound at her side. There was a wound around the kidney area. There was a wound to her upper abdomen. There were other wounds. The scars were whitish, older. As serendipity would have it, we were about to read the appearance to Thomas in scripture. I prepared to try to reach into those wounds. The call, I thought to myself, of Christ in the world is alive. "When I was recovering in hospital after the stabbing," said Del, "I got addicted to morphine and had to withdraw just like from heroin. I walked by the kid who attacked me. He'd been let out after only a matter of months because he was a minor."

Del figured she survived because she was so drunk that the blood pooled and she fell to the side, the side with the wound.

Every day even now another attack threatened. Yet Del was smiling more and played a concert on Miles Davis's birthday. She began to be our morning sound technician. The church became familiar to her. She said she considered me one of her few friends. The place had become a haven for her. Del would come over after the evening service from time to time and have some of my homemade wine. Knowing Del's predilection for self-destruction, I watched warily. This arrangement seemed to be safe for both of us. After all, this was exactly the relationship I had with a number of our congregants who would drop into the manse for chats or prayer. A queer form of evangelism, I thought?

> Del: I wanted to join a group at the health clinic speaking about sexual abuse. But they wouldn't let me in because I was "male." I demanded an apology but, of course, never got one. I was raised a Christian, you know. I'm still a recovering Christian. They (the Christians) hated me. I hate them. Being in this church is weird. There isn't any other church that I could stand being in for a minute.

And always the disclaimer:

> This is all just a conversation. Tomorrow it won't exist.

And we continued to worship, sing, speak, debate as Christians together. I began to see that it was, as *Christians*, together. Why else would we be together?

> Del: It came over me the other night that my father was dead. I haven't seen him in years and have no wish to see him. Yet somehow I just knew he had died. I'm sort of curious to know if that is so, but it's only curiosity.

And another time:

> Del: Here is the place in Deuteronomy I was telling you about. The place that deals with homosexuality.
>
> Cheri: There are many places, but is it really homosexuality they're dealing with?
>
> Del: So what do you do with this?
>
> Cheri: I think it's bullshit. Everyone has their canon within canon. Martin Luther described the epistle of James as an epistle of "straw."
>
> Del: Cool.

And so, Bible study began.

Del came to Godtalk (our Bible study) and sat next to morning and evening service people and felt at home. I began to see evangelism as a call to me rather than a call from me to someone else. My call may be to listen to the gospel preached in the person of the other, particularly the other as marginalized. I learned this in Bible study.

Del also still needed to be fed, as poverty was her reality. We had found a friend.

When our normal musician was absent for evening services, Del began to willingly step in and play. With her musical ability, Del picked up the hymns quickly and one evening voiced an interest in playing or working with children. That is how Del became the music director for our vacation Bible camp.

> Del: I've gone off Prozac. It was making me depressed, it wasn't helping anymore, and I feel a hundred percent better.

It seemed true. Del was more energetic and seemed happier. She began to speak of getting back into playing music professionally.

> Del: I'm looking into paying gigs. I've been jamming some Reggae, and every so often we just hit this righteous groove. I need to reestablish myself.

> Cheri: It's kind of difficult if bookings can't reach you. You need a phone service.

> Del: I know, but I have no credit rating, and with my income it's never going to happen.

> Cheri: How much do you live on?

> Del: About five hundred a month.

Finally, a use for the benevolent fund that made sense, I thought. Direct aid for someone we knew to be both deserving and in need. We bought her a pay-as-you-go cell phone as payment for the vacation Bible camp.

Del was invited to my birthday party. She didn't come. I was more disappointed in not seeing her than some closer friends and relatives. I saw Del at the next service. To my memory Del had never missed an evening service.

> Del: Happy birthday. Sorry I missed your bash.

> Cheri: That's okay, we missed you.

> Del: Can I talk to you?

> Cheri: Sure...

We went to my office.

> Del: I didn't make it to your party because I was so messed up I physically just couldn't.

Cheri: What happened?

Del: I got my check, and, you know, when you're as grindingly poor as I am, you just want to blow some of it to forget you're so damn poor.

Cheri: I can believe that.

Del: So I went out for a few beers and got this jones and then went and got an eighty-dollar rock [crack cocaine] and just felt like shit the next day.

Cheri: But that was it...?

Del: Oh yeah, I mean I don't even like speed. It was just one of those stupid things.

Cheri: Del, I hope so because I mean in a sense you're starting to be on the church's payroll....

Del: Shit, I knew I shouldn't tell you. I haven't told anyone else...shit, I knew....I hate it when middle-class people are down on poor people for getting stoned occasionally....I mean you've just got to escape....I told you it was a onetime, stupid thing....

Del seemed to recoil, pull in. I sensed my own inner panic....What if Del didn't/couldn't confide in me? What if I'd blown it? Damn it, I'd been judgmental and morally judgmental at that. Where had all my counseling training gone?

Cheri: Sorry, Del. You know, it's just that we deal with so much crack addiction around here....It's scary!

Del: No hay, no harm...I mean addicts. I mean I've seen people sit around do five hundred in a night....Don't worry...won't happen. I'm too old for that shit.

We ended well. Del played that night. We spoke. We made plans. I wondered how codependent I was being, or had I been taught an incredibly valuable lesson in humility?

The evening service was and is often interrupted with what I call "the prophets." Individuals with schizophrenia or just something to say and nowhere to say it will enter and speak out loud during the service. It has been our practice from the beginning to acknowledge them, give them space, offer them the dignity of listening but with a time limit so that others may worship or say their piece too. In my interaction that night with Del, I felt as I sometimes did with the prophets, as though listening was a more profound form of worship. I still don't know what my correct response should have been or not been. I admitted that in ministry I very rarely know what my correct response should or should not be. Very rarely if ever do I know what Christ would have me do. Now it strikes me as arrogance to ever claim anything close to certainty.

In the most commonplace and mundane of ministerial encounters I felt and feel the undecidability of the call and of any ethical imperative. Increasingly, I fell back on standard counseling practices of listening nonjudgmentally and pointing out participants' own inconsistencies. But as I do it I notice that the healing that occurs, if any, runs both ways. I felt that my own uncovered fears around abandonment and failure were also lessening. Perhaps a better way of describing the encounter is that both of us became aware of the presence of the Holy Spirit and we both eventually shut up.

It was the first in many lessons in evangelism delivered to me by Del.

Another's Beginnings

Years after Emmanuel Howard Park's early experiences as church with trans folk and with Del, I read a book that would have assisted our journey: *Transgendered: Theology, Ministry, and Communities of Faith* written by Justin Tanis. He wrote about the signs of a welcoming transpositive church: genuine hospitality, nondiscrimination policies and attitudes, appropriate and inclusive language, the visible and audible presence of trans people and programs, provision of meaningful rituals to mark changes, outreach to trans groups and individuals, opportunities for the congregation to learn accurately about trans issues, and restrooms that the gender-variant can access.[5]

Tanis also wrote about gender as a "calling":

> I believe for a number of reasons that the lens of calling is a useful and relevant way to look at gender. One of those reasons is that it does make us look at the divine role in our gender and brings it forward as a positive part of our gender identity. Rather than simply being a fluke, an oddity, or a source of shame, gender variance comes to be seen as

---

5. Justin Tanis, *Transgendered: Theology, Ministry, and Communities of Faith* (Cleveland: Pilgrim Press, 2003), 122.

part of our God-given identities. Even more than that, it becomes our spiritual responsibility to explore fully the nature that God has given to us. Like a calling, our sense of our own genders arises within us and, at the same time, seems to come from a source that is beyond our control or volition. The sense of our own genders arises from within and without, from us and beyond us. We know it in our innermost beings, and it comes from a source that is greater than we alone.[6]

As Del and I walked, there seemed to be no route maps, no lists of what we needed to do as community, no understanding in church literature, never mind literature on evangelism to guide us. She was the prophet, the advanced guard of a new way of being that demanded of our church and me a process of education that we would never have known we needed but for her. We could do nothing but follow her lead. Her "call" as transgendered became our community's "call" as church. She gave us purpose. Our purpose was to welcome her and through her all queerness everywhere.

Tanis again:

> We need to do this for transgendered people so that we might live freely and fully, but we also need to take this stand for nontransgendered people. They need freedom from the strict gender policing of our society. They need to feel able to make radical changes in their lives simply because such change is the right thing for them to do. I am convinced that one reason that people become enraged and frightened of us is because we have the courage to change something fundamental about ourselves in order to become more fully realized human beings, more joyful people. That freedom and courage scares people, and pushes buttons for many, but that path is the road to liberation.[7]

Or, one might want to add, the road to the cross, which is not necessarily more joyful but is certainly more Christian.

We, as nontransgendered folk, struggled with using "she" and "her" when referencing Del. We shared bedrooms on women's retreats. We invited opening discussion of trans issues on those same retreats so that the nontrans women might understand the presence of those in our midst that seemed more male. Our straight working-class men, whatever threat they might have felt, generously agreed to act "as if"

---

6. Ibid., 149.
7. Ibid., 185.

they were comfortable around our increasing population of trans folk while at church.

I heard judgment from unlikely sources, like lesbian women: "If she wants to claim the status of 'woman,' then she should dress as a woman at least," in reference to Del. I'm sure there was also much discussion in households of the church that were judgmental. The profound and holy miracle, however, was that even those who were confused by the new faces (and bodies) understood the concept of "sanctuary."

Justin Tanis again:

> Your congregation may be the one place, outside of a person's home, where she or he can be genuinely themselves. You may provide a very meaningful opportunity for self expression to a cross dresser by creating a safe and respectful environment in which that individual can dress as he or she wishes to dress. Perhaps your congregation can be the place where someone tests out a new name and new pronouns to see how they feel. A faith community can become literally a sanctuary in which a trans person is able to feel safe, whole, and dignified.[8]

We also needed a place that was safe for the questions of children and the presence of children's questions (when it came to transgender issues, we were all children). One of our members, a young woman with Down syndrome who had a fast friendship with one of our trans members (male-to-female), overheard a discussion about the trans status of her friend. "What is a transsexual?" she asked timidly.

Her friend explained, "I was born in a man's body but I'm really a woman, so now I dress as a woman and take hormones to make me more of a woman and one day may have an operation to make me a woman physically."

Her honest and childish immediate reaction was, "That's gross!" upon which she corrected herself: "I mean you're my best friend and everything, I don't mean to say anything wrong."

We all laughed at the sheer honesty of the exchange. Our trans member responded, "The important thing is that I love you and you love me, don't you think?"

---

8. Ibid., 122.

In such simple and open ways, an astounding education was unfolding, an incredible discipleship, a miraculous Christian formation.

Looking back, Del's presence among us as angel and prophet, Del's presence among us as the queerest of the queer, was a complete and utter gift. We really had done little to "deserve" it, even by being statedly affirming and inclusive. She then made it possible for others to come and feel welcome. Yet even Del was not the reason the other trans folk came.

In retrospect, I am often asked how we attracted trans folk, and the best I can offer is that we did not discourage trans folk. We came to see them as the queerest of the queer, the prophetic voices of a new way of being Christian, of understanding Christian, and of being church, but that was their message to us, not our message to them. The Holy Spirit acted upon our community in this way. We were passive and willing participants in an active evangelization movement.

A new stained-glass window is being added as I write. Next to the pictures of the disciples created in the twenties when the church was built, next to the biblical scenes of Christ's parables and Hebrew prophets, next to the dedications of those lost from the congregation during multiple wars, will be placed a picture of Del (now deceased). She will be captured as she was, long graying hair in a ponytail, features possibly but not really Native, face in a characteristic and ironic half-smile, visage both male and female. There is only one other stained-glass window in the nave that could be called transgendered, one other saint of the church that exhibits both male and female characteristics. That is the classic countenance of the disciple John, the one whom Jesus loved, looking completely feminine at the stained-glass rendition of the Last Supper.

Chapter Five

Qu(e)erying Acts

At the Beginning

Queers like Del were attending the morning service, as well as the evening service, and queers unlike Del were proliferating. People started confiding in me all the secrets of their lives, not to be absolved but so as, in a sense, to see if it were possible for them to absolve the church enough to continue attending. Many had toxic religious backgrounds.

Mary, for example, a transsexual (so defined, in Mary's case, no surgery or hormones, just women's clothes) who came in drag every night when s/he wasn't in jail for cocaine use, changed her name from Marion back to her original "Mary" because it was her "real" name. Marion was an interesting name because it was unisexual, s/he said, but Mary was what she was born with — what she was born with being different, of course, from what her parents named her. S/he had been laughed at as she tripped over the edge of a carpet in another church's service. S/he had grown up with elders coming to her house praying over her as s/he insisted on wearing women's clothes. It was Mary's pastor who had suggested to her parents that she be institutionalized at thirteen.

Many of the homeless we saw were ambiguous as to sexual preference. I began to learn that many of the traditional morning service Christians had secrets both sexual and otherwise that had been "judged" by some clergy person or religious institution. In a similar vein, our growing edge in the morning became young couples, often with young children, who were not allowed to marry in their birth denominations or who had no intention of marrying for now and did not want to be sanctioned.

Many women had abortions and wanted to know if our church condemned them for it. Most, if not all, had had sex before marriage and wanted to know if that meant they were "sinful." Christianity had become synonymous in many of their minds with sexual judgment, with morality.

I learned[1] that five babies a day in North America alone are born with both genitals, called "intersexual" by the medical establishment, and that surgically they were usually made into women, a procedure that is very similar to castration. I met a pantheon of sexual preferences and sexual personas and sexual beings in my day-to-day ministry and more as I gained credibility as someone "you could talk to."

The day-to-day church ran like most Protestant churches. We tried various ways of responding to the needs of our congregants and of being relevant to our community. The older members were astoundingly generous (Christian, one might say) with the strange new members. They were also grateful to have more people help out so they themselves didn't have to work so hard just to keep the place afloat.

We used some suggestions from church-growth advocates to encourage individual ministries. Retreat days, weekends, "Intro to Christianity" days, Family Games nights, Parents and Tots drop-in, and small-group activities of various sorts emerged. Yet the composition of the groups that were started looked vastly different from other churches. We had "bag ladies" at Family Games nights. We had homeless persons and crack addicts on our retreats. We had schizophrenic, transsexual drug users at our "Intro to Christianity" seminars.

There was no question that we numbered among us some of our city's most marginalized. The question became: "How to be church for *them?*" We had a working definition of Christian as "anyone who defines herself/himself as Christian is a Christian." This had various ramifications.

"Anyone who wants to come to Communion is welcome." I was reminded of a professor's question to me awhile back: "Would you include a Muslim at the Eucharist?" In our church we would and did, if the Muslim wanted to participate.

---

1. *Sex TV*, Broadcast City TV, Toronto, January 15, 2001.

The motive was always to be found by the marginalized and be cared for by them. To care for the marginalized seemed biblical to us. Christ came, healed, called, commissioned. He seemed to respond to those who had the faith to call upon him to respond. So did we call upon him. Christianity was not about holding correct doctrine. If it were, those among our congregation who had brain damage or were psychiatric survivors would have been excluded. It was not about living a "clean" life, whatever that might mean, because if it were, those of our congregation who were prostitutes would have been excluded.

The radical inclusivity which seemed to be Christ's way was the way we wished to follow. And remember that "we" included all manner of marginalized, including the above mentioned. It also included middle-class, professional, doctors, lawyers, advertising executives, film producers, accountants, and a myriad of other professions. "Difference" was a challenge to everyone. We preached about it constantly, we lived it constantly, and we attempted to deal with the upheavals lovingly.

Given this congregation, sin was spoken of in terms of original sin, that is, in terms of our all being in Adam, rather than in terms in which some could judge others. We discussed it as "separation from God," a state into which we are born. This was scripturally, theologically, and philosophically based but also simply love for those in our midst. We tried to feed the sheep and counted on sins being covered by God's mercy. The sheep fed us, and we counted on our sins being covered by God's mercy. The sheep's proclivities we left to God.

This, of course, is nothing new to a Christian church. What was new, if anything, was the we/them dichotomy. "We," including leaders, were increasingly "them." I, as Ordered Minister, began to look again at theories, books, and theologies that dealt with "them." Anything that would hurt those who had already been wounded by the world was discarded. Anything that reeked of human judgment, especially of a "moral" nature, was discarded. This included the "morality" that saw itself as too righteous to be welcoming of a fairly right-wing youth group who came to stay in our basement and do "mission" work among us. Or of two young homesick elders of the Church of Jesus Christ of Latter-day Saints (Mormons) who came to dinner and then tried to convert our evening service en masse. We welcomed them into the service, where they read scripture and took Communion. We heard the apostle Paul's comments about queers. Queers among us took it, as Mary said, "That he was just a man of his time, although loveable in many other ways."

We represented a large range of theological opinion. Our evening services were almost Pentecostal in form. There was spontaneous prayer and clapping and bouncy singing and overheads. Our morning service was more traditional, with classically trained soloists and prepared bulletins. We included some very morally self-righteous individuals. They were never unloved, but welcomed and debated with.

"God hates homosexuals!" said a young man on welfare one night.

"No, God doesn't. I'm homosexual and he loves me!" responded another from our Outreach Committee.

"God may love you, but he hates your sin!" insisted the young man.

"But I *am* a homosexual and a sinner and Jesus died for me! Would you like me to take your plate? You're kinda cute, you know!"

"Do you really think so?" said the young man with genuine interest in the reaction. That was the end of the discussion. But they both kept coming back.

The evening service became the cause célèbre of our congregation at Emmanuel Howard Park, and many members in response to a stewardship drive earmarked their offerings for the work of the evening service. Yet the evening service "work" was really the work of the whole church. By mistake or by the Holy Spirit, younger unchurched folk wandered into our evening service and were impressed by the love and deep spirituality it represented and then ended up either staying there or gravitating to the morning service if they had kids or simply felt more comfortable with the morning worship.

My Sundays became marathons from early morning to late at night. Dinners needed to be started around 3:00 p.m. And people started arriving as soon as they could to hang out. Some would come to get off the streets. Almost all came to the service even though they didn't need to; it was never a requirement. Instead of delivering a prepared sermon I asked if anyone had something they wanted me to address, and many brought their own meditations and prayers. I started to tell the scriptural stories in my own words because I noticed the attention went up when I did. The Lord's Supper was served by different congregants each Sunday.

Most of my ministry and their ministry to me happened over coffee before the service. It took a long while for many to trust church or a church person at all. When they could, they did. When I left for vacation, there was always someone to take over for me.

For the first many months we struggled along singing without accompaniment. We decided to pray for a piano player. One day a guest baritone in the morning service offered to come and help out one evening. A talented musician and clergy person, he stayed and became part-time staff. It was a powerful example of love to those who had been taught that God didn't care about them.

New people came, invited by our members. One woman, Jane, invited a number of new people who became more involved. Don, an elderly gentleman, brought several people. Del brought a number. Many became members of our Outreach Committee.

We lost some too. Often this was a positive sign. Two crack addicts, who had been working on diminishing their intake, needed to leave the area and ended up going home to help themselves recover. Two prison ministries (an individual and an ecumenical group) became associated with the church.

I performed relationship blessings. These were of those who were queer or of those who simply had lost their papers or couldn't afford a license, and couldn't afford to get a divorce. All were invited to our premarriage class. Again the operative biblical imperative was "no human judgment." We saw these unions to be just as joyous as more traditional weddings and took them as seriously as any other covenant. The state became less and less important in the occasion.

Repentance was held up as important, as it is biblically, but we interpreted this as turning to Christ. Christ's love came first, and repentance followed. If repentance and conversion didn't happen, we were pleased nonetheless that people kept coming back so that Christ's love could be celebrated. We felt — and knew biblically — that conversion was up to God, not us.

The priesthood of all believers was a foundational belief. We understood that we all had different gifts and didn't see them as being part of a hierarchy. I preached and coordinated worship, but sometimes others preached and coordinated. My image in their eyes, as Del said, was "as mother." As mother, I tried to be a provider and dependable in love. Those were my gifts. We, in leadership, tried to dispel anything that seemed self-congratulatory by telling our own stories of failure and addiction.

We lived a denial of the priesthood as hierarchy, as being in any way more "moral" than laity. We lived a denial of this as a new kind of morality by preaching a kind of antisanctimonious line. None of this was meant to be popular, and little of it was. Our numbers were growing, but no coterie of disciples around anyone developed, nor would it later. I saw myself as living a kind of penance for being clergy. I presided over the Lord's Supper because I knew the lines and did it best. I wore the traditional alb and stole because our evening service congregants and morning congregants liked it. For many the sight of a woman in such garb represented queerness anyway.

Some nights we had 20, one night 114, most nights 30 to 40. Our sanctuary still looked more empty than full, and even our morning congregation, which looked fuller, still paled in comparison to our Roman Catholic neighbors on either side. I struggled daily with feelings of failure around this, which I interpreted as being a lack of faith. I thought often of the early church and reminded myself that numbers did not equal evangelism. I thought often of Stephen Neill's analysis that the church had only grown by a sort of imperialism, or by monasticism or martyrdom. I tried to see ourselves as a new sort of martyrdom or retreat/monasticism.[2]

Then I wondered why I was so enamored of the idea of the growth of the church at all. Institutionally I realized how necessary it was both for our denomination and our local church, but biblically I wasn't so sure. Evangelism as the sharing of the good news of Jesus Christ was the imperative. Wasn't the result of that evangelism God's prerogative? Wasn't evangelism itself God's prerogative?

The evening service and its participants left little time for theological musings. Mostly there were practical matters to attend to. There were many crises, needs, calls. I began to feel that the response to the

---

2. Stephen Neill, *A History of Christian Missions* (London: Penguin, 1984), 57.

calls that came was the operative theology, a beginning that seemed to do with the ethical imperative left after moral judgment abated.

"Bad dates," persons who solicited our prostitutes and then hurt them or stole from them, were a neighborhood problem. Squeegy kids were being ticketed by the police. And some of our crack addicts who were working on diminishing their abuse were still being arrested and jailed, halting their progress. All of these issues seemed to need a new kind of response.

We became involved with other local initiatives: banking projects to free up access for low-income people, food banks, and university radio. These were ways of serving our congregants by being a voice in the wider political arena. Questions of morality were always the first from the lips of anyone secular when they asked questions of what went on in our church.

The story in Acts of Philip baptizing the Ethiopian eunuch was often invoked in discussions. The first foreign, completely Gentile, convert was one of the most sexually marginalized of her/his day. Del commented on it and went out and told others about it. "What is to prevent me from being baptized?" (Acts 8:36) became the question. And if baptism, why not marriage, Eucharist, ordination?

My struggles with making time for my own family and other pursuits were no different than my congregants', although I was vastly more privileged. Money was always a church issue, as it was at all of the evening services and mine. I had a vested interest in the church surviving and a fervent desire for it to survive. Its survival required money. We struggled to be generous with each other. The first evening we took up a collection, the generosity from the participants made me cry.

Church growth usually meant growth in giving, or at least that was what I had learned at seminary. Yet growing a church with the poor was no guarantee of that. In fact, it might cost more. Despite the generosity of the evening service, they would never be able to fund the physical plant, the salaried staff, even the food. I noticed that our finance committee was not impressed by the growing evening service. Was the desire for church growth really a desire for more givings in most churches?

I began saying to people who asked about this research, "It has to do with the issue of evangelism and church growth. If all you want to do is grow a church and you don't care about the money, just feed people and they will come." But even talk of getting people to come began to ring hollow. Getting people to do something wasn't "it." Increasingly, getting myself to define what "it" — evangelism — is in terms of my doing something wasn't working either. What was evangelism? What was its movement in and out of our church? Was the good news of Jesus Christ a phrase that needed to be acceded to? Was it an action that needed to be done? Was it something that could be given or even communicated at all? Was what was happening in my ministry in any way evangelical? Was defining evangelism a question that could even be answered? Could it even be posed correctly?

We had begun with a radical inclusivity that did not demand that people lie or change to be fed either food or scripture. We examined biblical and theoretical roots to ascertain the queerness of scripture and the queerness of the one who was both proclaimer and content of scripture, Christ. We found no New Testament warrants for human judgment and professed our alignment with the reformer's foundation, *sola scriptura*. We also aimed at assisting all those who struggled in parishes with inclusivity as their mandate as they lived the day-to-day of ministry. How was one to follow faithfully?

Like the people in Acts, like the Ethiopian eunuch, we had heard the word preached, we had been moved, we had seen the word's effects on others. We had felt the communal strength and love of Christian community. We could not think of another community that existed on love in quite that way. We had been fed, physically and spiritually. We didn't feel comfortable, or Christian, unless we extended the same to others. To us, this was called "loving your neighbor." We had been changed and changed our lives, but it most certainly was not a gift bestowed upon us from the other but from the Other.

An Earlier Beginning

In Acts, as in the gospels, there is a terrific movement of dissemination, beginning with about 120 (Acts 1:15). This becomes many and then scatters with persecution (Acts 6:7; 8:1). In this way the early church's movement was like the movement of Israel, scattered and regrouped to be scattered again.

The early church shared resources, and its members helped each other directly and substantially (Acts 3:44–46). They preached everywhere and often, most often in places where the message was in danger of falling on unreceptive ears (e.g., Acts 8:4). They healed as often as they preached throughout Acts. But interestingly, the descriptions of conversions to the new Christian faith are a list of individuals. It seemed important to the author of Acts that the individual names be known and celebrated and that their stories be told.

So we learn of the Ethiopian, of Saul who becomes Paul, of Tabitha and Aeneas, Cornelius, Ananias, and on and on. Most are converted by some healing miracle, we are told. They are made whole and then sent forth. They go virtually all over the world as it was known to the ancients. Small churches were established. Risks were taken. The results were always the same: persecution and death.

If church evangelism has to do with the movement of Acts, it has to do with healing, telling the story of Jesus Christ, and the radical redistribution of goods. It does not necessarily result in increased numbers because of history or demography. In fact, the only sure result is the death of the disciple, as most met imprisonment and execution. It also seems to have to do with a sort of "one person at a time" approach. It seems important to the dissemination of the Word that one life at a time be changed. Certain lives have a noteworthy importance in terms of their use for the dissemination or evangelization process, Paul's for example.

Paul, the great evangelist, was a Roman citizen and persecutor of the Christians. It seemed important that someone so clearly antithetical to the young church be converted. It seemed important to God. God, in Acts and elsewhere in scripture, seems to work through the most unlikely candidates. The movement is from God to Paul. No human is involved. Even Ananias has to be sent by God to Saul/Paul. He most certainly wants nothing to do with this enemy on his own. Ananias goes grudgingly and heals only because he has been sent against his will. The result is the most famous new Christian of them all, a Christian not converted by another Christian but by God.

It is as if the movement of conversion is that preachers are brought those who need healing that are already converted. Evangelism consists of being there. In Acts it is a passive/active act: passive because it accomplishes nothing God has not already done, and active because a great deal of energy is spent in traveling, preaching, and healing, even though these activities do not in themselves bring about the conversion of anyone. Preaching and healing to all and sundry is what the disciples of the early church are called to do in Acts because they are obedient. They are called to obedience, however imperfect. Conversion happens in spite of them, around them, but never directly because of them. The role of speaking the "good news," as in Romans 10:14–17, is one often performed reluctantly.

This bears repeating. The biblical testament is that God calls to faith and calls the faithful. God converts. Whether transcendent or immanently through humans, the movement always begins with God. Human creatures, simply in their obedience, preach, heal, and travel. They also are healed and preached to. But they do not convert. The act of evangelism is an act of obedience to God and is rife with all the problems humans have with humans (the epistles address some of those problems) and has a minimum to do with engendering faith (Paul may very well have heard about Jesus from the Christians he persecuted). Acts makes clear that humans have no power in this regard. Jesus uses earthen vessels, sending out the apostles as evangelists (Matt. 28:19), but the movement always commences with Christ or God.

Acts also makes clear that death and the destruction of Christian community is a much more likely outcome of evangelism in the above sense than church growth. And the impetus for evangelism comes from the one evangelized. The Ethiopian searches out the one with the good news because s/he as an individual has been sent, in a very real way, from God.

The outpouring of the Holy Spirit on Gentiles comes as a shock to everyone at Pentecost, and it occasions the early rift within the infant Christian communities. Paul's struggle is to accept and convince others to accept Gentiles into the chosen people. Eugene Rogers Jr. writes:

> The formula of Galatians 3:28 (*There is neither Jew nor Greek, slave nor free, male nor female, for you are all one in Christ Jesus.*) confirms Paul's experience of and conforms it to a baptismal practice. It is first of all a description of the eschatological community in which Gentiles become

part of God's holy nation without first becoming Jews. . . . Especially for
a Church composed almost entirely of Gentiles, the formula is to be
taken as a warning, even a threat.[3]

Again God pours God's Spirit out upon, for the Christian communities, the most unlikely people, people like Paul, people like the
Gentiles, people like queers (the eunuch). Scripture demonstrates that
Jews were the true people of God and that those who were considered
morally suspect, like the Gentiles, were accepted with enormous re-
luctance. God's morality is not the human creature's morality. God's
idea of who is to be added to the Christian community is the someone
that the Christian community often pointedly fears and hates.

The biblical paradigm may be that it is the one who is hated who
wants to become Christian. It is the someone who is hated who has
been sent by God to the Christian community, to test the community's
faithfulness. It can be argued at this point that the true evangelist is
the outsider who asks to be let in. Paul, as prototypical evangelist,
was the hated other who was sent by God to a frightened church
(Ananias). In a sense Paul never left that role, as the letters he wrote
spoke of his constant efforts to let the outsider in.

It could be argued that the one sent by God has more, not less, right
and credibility to the title "Christian" than the ones called church.
Such a one is the current prophet calling the church ever back to
obedience. The one from outside the temple, like Christ, like Paul, is
the one from God. The church's role is to find that voice so that it
can find its own raison d'être. By preaching, healing, and traveling,
by flinging the doors of the temple open wide, the church hopes to
find the one whose voice will call it (the church) back to obedience,
an obedience from which it is always defecting.

Should we then be both passively and actively looking for the one
who comes from God, the one hated, the one whose hallmarks will
most likely elicit our moral repugnance? Christ, by this measure, is
never comfortable in the temple but only knocking at the door. The
movement of evangelism is a movement to the constituted Christian
community. The community is the recipient of the movement, not
its originator. Faithfulness is always more likely found outside in the

---

3. Eugene Rogers Jr., *Sexuality and the Christian Body* (Oxford: Blackwell, 1999), 66.

question "What is to prevent me from being baptized?" than in the community's response.

The gift is given by God, always Other, breaking into the circle from the outside. The church's action is to accept or reject, to "give economy its chance" as Derrida would say, to give the circle a new spin or to become monologic, to refuse the gift and gift giving, to keep the barriers raised. There is either every moral reason not to baptize or only one reason to baptize. God requests baptism. The evangelical movement calls for a "Yes!!" in response to God's request.

The expansion of the church, in Stephen Neill's schema, by monasticism, martyrdom, or imperialism then is irrelevant except insofar as it is a reflection of the church's response to God's request. If there is a request, so be it. If not, not.

Homosexuals' request for ordination, women's request for ordination, or any other outside (queer) request for inclusion is therefore impossible to deny where God has sent the outsider to the church. The responsibility and fault would then lie with the church, and the question is not, "Should the church forgive homosexuals?" but "Can queers who are sent forgive the church?" The church should in that case wait prayerfully and repentantly for *its* forgiveness.

Should we then ordain pedophiles and axe murderers? Anyone and everyone who seeks baptism, inclusion in the church, should receive it if the request comes from God. Is ordination the raising up of an individual or the servanthood of an individual? Should the most morally heinous be allowed to serve the church? It is similar to the question of keeping sinners from church. Obviously in the world this is unlikely to happen because judgment is so swift and so moral, especially self-judgment. But if we remind ourselves of Acts, we remind ourselves of one man named Paul who killed Jewish Christians one day and preached the gospel on a day soon after.

The Ethiopian eunuch was a morally reprehensible persona in the ancient world of the Jews. S/he was unclean, foreign, sexually ambiguous. S/he went on her/his way rejoicing after receiving inclusion in the Christian community; presumably s/he too was now an evangelist. S/he too now preached the good news of Jesus Christ.

Obviously, as Paul outlines, we all have different gifts, and not all are called to ordained ministry. Some may simply be delusional and not prophetic. But discernment is both an act of the church or Christian community and the individual. Worthiness and readiness are questions to be asked in every baptism and every ordination, *of the church.* Underlying every judgment by the church should be the memory of Paul, murderer, blind, Roman, possibly delusional, and that Ananias laid hands upon him in a gesture that could only be baptism and ordination.

Imagining ourselves evangelists, as Paul was, what then is the call of the evangelist? To review, to listen for God's call, to accept healing, to accept baptism, to assist others in their ministries, to receive others and never to refuse God's request. Whether it comes as a bolt from above or a still, small voice, the results and actions are the same.

Back Home Again

We found ourselves doing these things at the evening service and the morning service for the queerest of the queer, souls so queer that some queers found them unacceptable. Evangelism occurred in the listening to the queerest of the queer, sent from God. The requests of God and from God came through people, people like Del.

Del became the test case. Could we heed God's call from Del? Could we be inclusive enough to include her ministry? So began the saga. I asked if she would object if our conversations became the sort that would have a structure, that could be analyzed so that my bias could be monitored. Could I prove obedient enough to love her at the end of it all? That was the test case for my church's conversion. Could we include her in our community? Would she forgive us enough to allow this to happen?

Following are the questions around which our conversation hovered. I also interviewed Mary and the others, queer in a parallel way for the same reasons, with similar questions over a shorter period. A journey had begun.

Chapter Six

Qu(e)erying Genesis

Our Beginning

There is a genesis to qu(e)erying. We hoped to remain scripturally faithful, and therefore qu(e)erying Genesis should seem to be our beginning. Should we welcome Del with a view to changing her, or should we change to welcome Del? What did scripture say to this? Were humans created androgynously? In Genesis 1:27, were humans created androgynous in the first instance? Literally first as in scripturally first. The verse states in its original:

> *Va-yivra' 'elohim 'et ha-adam be-tzalmo, be-tzelem 'elohim bara' 'oto, zakhar u-nequvah bara' 'otam,* and God created the man in his image, in the image of God he created him (*'oto,* masculine singular, matching the gender of the noun "adam"), male and female he created them (*'otam,* masculine plural this time, which can be used for sets of nouns which include masculine and feminine nouns).[1]

Sally Gross, in an article titled "Intersexuality and Scripture," quotes from Rabbi Yirmiyah (Jeremiah) ben "El'azar."

> When the Holy One Blessed be He created the primal man (the primal Adam), He created him an androgyne, and it is therefore said: "male and female he created them." (Bereshit Rabbah)[2]

She points out that in the Talmud a tradition is contained which even points to Abraham and Sarah as being intersexed. She quotes:

> Abraham and Sarah were (each of them a) *tumtum* as it is said: "Look to the rock from which you were hewn, and the quarry from which you

---

1. Sally Gross, "Intersexuality and Scripture" (*www.bfpubs.demon.co.uk/sally.htm.*)
2. Ibid.

were digged" (Isaiah 51:1) and it is written: "Look to Abraham your father and to Sarah who bore you" (Isaiah 51:2). Rabbi Nahman said in the name of Rabbah bar Abuha: Sarah our mother was an *'aylonith*, as it is said: "Now Sarah was barren; and she had no child" (Genesis 11:30) — she did not have a womb.[3]

Gross points out there is a clear understanding of ambiguous sexuality in the Talmud and its place in scripture. In Numbers 5:3 the phrase which is usually translated as male and female as distinct dichotomies is in Hebrew more of an indication of a continuum, more "from male to female" (*mi-zakhar ve-'ad neqevah*).

In the Renaissance, hermaphroditism was seen as a mark of wholeness, this from the Rabbinic gloss on Genesis 1:27, an original perfection that was somehow lost. One, Rabbi Shmuel bar Nahman, also suggested because of the syntactic ambiguity that Adam was Janus faced, male on one side and female on the other. In this he was similar to the Midrash Berreshit Rabbah 8.

In the second story in Genesis, the story of Eve formed by Adam's rib, *tselah* translated as rib is used elsewhere to refer to a section or wing (as in the wing of a building) or half of a structure. Adam did not lose a small unnecessary bone but a substantial part of himself in the splitting of himself into Eve.

Hermaphroditism predates Adam's sin, Gross asserts, and she further points out that the genital reconstruction that happens so often with intersexed infants is decidedly unbiblical (Deut. 23:1).[4]

I wondered when considering the number of genital reassignment surgeries performed whether intersexuality in its physical form and transgenderism in its psychic variety is not a variation of normal occurrence by any statistical standards? I wondered, as a Christian, even if it is considered a deformation, why there would be a negative morality attached to it? Do we consider morally repugnant the blind or the deaf?

Kathy Rudy does an interesting exegesis of another Genesis story, Sodom and Gomorrah.

3. Ibid.
4. Ibid.

The people of Sodom teach us that what is ultimately pleasing to God about our sexuality is hospitality. If our sexual relations help us open our hearts and our homes to lost travellers and needy strangers, they are good. And if they cause us to be aggressively territorial and abusive to outsiders, they are evil. Hospitality can be the new criterion by which we determine the morality of sexual acts. Rather than locating morality along lines of procreation, or along the lines of complementarity, we can now measure sexual morality by determining how well our sexual encounters help us welcome the stranger into our church and into our life with God. The original intent of ethical teachings about sexuality was to ensure that sex was pleasing to God by being open to new members joining the community of faith. Clearly, this can be accomplished by hospitality as well as by birth.[5]

The Christian principle behind sexual ethics for Rudy seems to be evangelism. Does the act of sex bring those involved to God? The principle of procreativity, as understood by moral theologians in the past, was, in a sense, an issue of the growth of the church. The principle of unitivity, uniting with other Christians in Christian community, also could be construed as evangelism. In the principle of complementarity, the gendered binaries of man/woman are seen as necessary whether procreation occurs or not, if we have the input of modernism over biblical mandate.

Complementarity is also anticommunal in the sense that the man/woman binary is a world in and of itself. The early Christian emphasis was on the Christian community as primary grouping as was the scriptural witness in the New Testament. Complementarity would seem to be guilty of the "idolatry" that Paul seemed to link with homosexual activity. If we have everything we need in the other, what need have we of the Other? Or, if together, man/woman are the image of God, what need do we have of Christ? Or if the reading of male and female in Genesis is not genitally resident, then why weren't the born intersexed simply a biological example of a human reality? Whatever male and female are, as genders, they can be resident in the reverse biologies or in one body.

Even if one disagrees with Gross's reading of biblical anthropology and the midrashic understandings cited, the question remains as

---

5. Kathy Rudy, *Sex and the Church* (Boston: Beacon, 1997), 126.

to what we mean when we, as contrasted with scripture, speak of male/female. One could argue that the sexually queer do not forsake the male/female binary so much as redefine it. Their existence points to another understanding of male/female that is not genitally fixed or fixated but perhaps even more originary than that.

Qu(e)erying has its own genesis as well. The move from arguing based on biological or determinist givens for leniency toward homo-sexuals by a self-righteous church[6] to a far more poststructuralist analysis is exemplified by the theologian Mary McClintock Fulkerson:

> What is troubling about this shared territory is the assumption of both positions (pro and con ordination of practicing homosexuals) that sex-ual identity is fundamental to persons' being, and that there are two kinds of sexual persons: heterosexual and homosexual. Although that does not lead to the same views of the relation between one's sex and one's desire, since the progressives are free to wonder if sexual orien-tation is fixed, the frame still assumes that anatomical sex and gender coincide in two types of subject, allowing for desire itself to be de-fined by difference. The definition of desire on this heterosexual grid means that the progressive position damns with faint praise the very subjects it wishes to liberate. As always the phenomenon that must be explained is not sexuality in all its complexities, but the veering off of a subject's desire from its proper binary opposite to its mirror image: the search is for the causes of homosexuality, never the causes of heterosexuality.[7]

She goes on to argue that as long as heterosexuality is seen as the norm, the best homosexuality can do is be as-good-as. This is really just her review of Judith Butler's work, but it is news that Butler has begun to influence theology. One can be entirely scripturally faithful and see the male and female creation as resident in varying degrees as gender, in both sexes.

There is an enormous volume of work that seeks to rationalize biblical passages seemingly about homosexuality. An example is the Student Christian Movement's pamphlet on the topic, which hits in a succinct manner the major stories quoted by some Christians. Genesis

---

6. For example, John Shelby Spong, *Living in Sin: A Bishop Rethinks Sexuality* (San Francisco: HarperSanFrancisco, 1990).

7. Mary McClintock Fulkerson, "Gender — Being It or Doing It? The Church, Homo-sexuality and the Politics of Identity," in *Que(e)rying Religion: A Critical Anthology,* ed. David Comstock and Susan E. Henking (New York: Continuum, 1997).

18:16–19:38, the story of Sodom and Gomorrah, does not condemn homosexuality but inhospitable behavior in their estimation. One can see by Rudy's work how "hospitality" itself can become the new mandate for a twenty-first-century moral theology.[8] Hence qu(e)erying has moved from defending against Genesis 18 to defending *from* Genesis 18.

In Leviticus 18:22 and 20:13, the Hebrew word *toevah*, which is translated as abomination, does not refer to an intrinsic evil such as rape or murder but to something unclean. Other abominations prohibit blended textiles, eating of pigs, seafood, etc. These codes were already hotly debated in the early church.

In Romans 1:26–27, Paul was concerned with idolatry. Same-sex activity in Greek and Roman society was reserved for the wealthy, and it usually meant pedophilia. To conform to the powerful and wealthy was to conform to hierarchy and not to God and Christian community. One can equally use the principle of "complementarity" to stand in for idolatry. We remind ourselves the most auspicious state to Paul was celibacy.[9]

Queer theology has been developing so as to proclaim scripture as pro-queer. It is perhaps time for "progressives," as Mary C. Fulkerson calls them (a term that seems to denote another kind of righteousness), to look to scripture for a *defense* of queerness, which it most certainly seems to be. This is, of course, different than a defense of homosexuality. To put it mildly, scripture seems to be a questioning of heterosexuality.

It is interesting when we look at the text as *body* that the text of Genesis is divided from itself. The text itself is ambiguous. The text as we earlier attempted to illustrate in the New Testament is queer. Midrash as exegesis is necessary because of its very queerness. Both textual and human bodies seem from God, in their originary, far from immediately decipherable. Or as Del said, "God is transgender," by which she meant that God has attributes of maleness and femaleness.[10] Exegesis is necessary, theology is necessary, because of

---

8. Rudy, *Sex and the Church.*
9. Student Christian Movement, *Homophobia in the Churches* (Toronto, 1999), 2.
10. Conversation with author, September 9, 2000.

the ambiguity of scripture. Canons within canons, also the work of theology, is necessary because of the contradictions, the breaks, and ruptures of scripture. Scripture as originary as text is still not originary, but its *truth*, if you will, is understood always and already in multiple translation.

God, also, is explicated to the church and through the church through scripture and doctrine. God is, for example, certainly three according to Christian doctrine: not three masks over one God, or three Gods, or one God only, all being heresies of the early church. The doctrine of the Trinity as truth is ambiguity as truth.

Defense itself is perhaps the wrong tactic of the queer enquiry. Perhaps the call is that queers need to evangelize the church. The church needs to be called back to faithfulness, a faithfulness to its own scripture from which it has strayed at the behest of modernism and of the world's powers. Perhaps in this century the church is the object of an evangelization process initiated by God and carried out by the queer.

Queers need to see themselves as first and foremost Christian, and Christians need to see themselves as queer. Kathy Rudy again:

> The command to be hospitable can be seen as a part of the great commission to tell the world the good news of Jesus Christ. Our task in reconstructing a progressive sexual ethic is not to deny or sidestep power, but rather to invite others into the power of God, to welcome them into the radically transformative power which realigns the world, to see each other as Christians rather than as men or women, gay or straight, rich or poor. The new standard of hospitality advocates a union with all needing persons and thus returns new life to the community. With hospitality, we have no way of condemning homosexuality because the very notion of same or different sex would fall away in favor of our common identification of Christian.[11]

It is worth noting that the familial structures of Jews at the time of Genesis and their notion of what family looked like was vastly different from anything we experience today. The average Hebrew household numbered closer to fifty or a hundred people, and there was little or no distinction between the public and private world. Families

---

11. Rudy, *Sex and the Church*, 128.

rather than individuals united, and whether husband and wife had any sentimentalized love or not, its existence was immaterial to the covenant bond.[12]

The genesis of the queer enquiry from a pleading at the door of power to an insistence that Christians were queer from the beginning becomes less a defense and more an insistence on a return to faithfulness and to Christian community and away from an idolatry of modernist notions of sex. Qu(e)erying becomes an orthodox move calling back (*religio*) to the roots and away from the world.

Our Beginning Again

The genesis of the qu(e)erying project in my congregation was to allow myself to be evangelized by queers, transgendered persons, the queerest of the queers, marginalized from homosexuals and heterosexuals and yet with the audacity to approach my congregation as if they belonged there. I began my interviews with a few key questions and then followed the conversation that developed in a semistructured way. Why did they pick this congregation at this time? What brought them here for the first time and what kept them coming back? What would stop them from being a member? What would keep them as members? How could the church serve them? What was their history with churches? What made them so queer? What did God mean to them? What did they think God's call to them was about? Who was Christ for them? How did they feel called by Christ to this place, or did they?

These were the critical things I needed to know. The purpose of my knowing was increasingly so that I could learn how to be more obedient. I fully expected that I might need to repent. I fully expected that I would learn more than I really wanted to know. I fully expected that the interviews would change and transform me. I needed conversion. To convert, I fully expected that I would need at many points to repent of my role and of my self.

---

12. Rodney Clapp, *Families at the Crossroads* (Downers Grove, Ill.: InterVarsity Press, 1993), 35–37.

I aimed to be hospitable. This required nonjudgment, both as to their biblical right to be a member of our congregation and also of my biblical right to be a member of my congregation. Expecting that I would hear judgment about the church from them, I aimed to listen and attempted to understand.

I aimed to try to understand a new nonbinary world, a world beyond gay and straight, male and female. Yet, human creatures being what we are, I wanted to stay sensitive to the new binaries around which righteous moral judgment might attach itself. Homophobe versus progressive might be one example. All meant all, even those that might want "all" to mean their own group. This, being impossible, became a vision to be aspired to rather than a dictum to be followed.

The difficulty at every turn would be to be inclusive, another word for hospitable. The ramifications for church in general and our congregation in particular were ever present. My image was one I used in marriage (union?) counseling. I aimed to stuff my judgments under my chair and be a listener only or as much as possible.

How We Began

The interviews took place in our sanctuary, which had become safe to all participants. I noted with irony that the sanctuary had at one time been perceived by many involved as unsafe. The interviews were held with just the two of us and a tape recorder in the room. I allowed all interviewees to hear and correct anything that they didn't really mean after recording. This also was recorded. Interviewees were allowed to read any transcripts and comment on my commentary and on any semifinished work. Their comments on the commentary would also be included if anything substantial was added.

It is important to note that a relationship had developed before any taping occurred. No taping could ever have occurred unless the relationship had existed prior to the project. The events and feelings were so personal and the participants' alienation from the church was so total that the project itself would never have come about otherwise. This was also part of the content of the interviews.

We spent many hours together before, during, and after the interviews, and therefore the transcripts are more a moment in an ongoing

Christian community, telling moments perhaps, but part of a greater continuum.

Included in the following chapter are the telling moments within the telling moments of the taped and coded and analyzed interviews, a sort of distillation of a relationship. I see it as a prescription for an ailing church, a church that has lost touch with its mandate to stand with the marginalized. It is a call to conversion from queers. It is queer evangelism.

Chapter Seven

A Guy Like Her — Mary

I first encountered Mary working our residential street. We lived on one of our inner-city neighborhood's most notorious "tracks" (a street on which prostitutes solicit clients). She was the most regular of all the sex trade workers and perhaps the best known. Mary was almost always high on crack cocaine, almost always working. I would sometimes see her early in the morning when the other "hookers" were absent and late at night.

Mary is perhaps six-foot-three, and in heels towers above most people. She is a native Canadian, bone thin, and always dressed in women's clothes. She has not had surgery but does take female hormones. She has no intention of having surgery, considering it too expensive and mutilating. She says she has always known that s/he was a woman, "from the earliest memory."

To the onlooker, Mary looked ill, too thin, had poor teeth and bruises. She was unwell, being HIV-positive and suffering from many smaller associated ailments. None of this seemed to keep her from working. Other hookers derided her and laughed at her. The few friends she made on the street would routinely become exhausted with her unreliability, lies, and occasional violence.

The police knew Mary well. She had a long string of petty arrests and more major felonies in her past, all of them directly or indirectly because of her crack addiction that was years in the making. Mary figured she'd always used drugs of some sort or another, beginning back in the sixties with abuse of alcohol and then moving on to heroin, crack, and prescription pharmaceuticals.

Mary was ageless looking but is in her forties. Some days she seemed much younger, others, much older. Her clients seemed to range in age as well, from older men to men with baby seats in the backs of their cars. It was often a matter of discussion among others in the congregation as to "who would pick her up?" stoned and sick as she often was. But clients did. Enough to keep her stoned and sick.

Astoundingly, she had only been in rehabilitation once and then only for a few months. Rehabilitation usually consisted of periods of imprisonment where her normal sources of supply would dry up. Our structured interview took place in prison where she was trying to secure a rehabilitation site that would keep her in for at least a year. As she said, "I need more time straight, more time away from the pressures of the street and the old circle of people."

Mary existed in my life for a long time before she ever walked into our church. I would pass her and say, "Hi!" She would always respond. Sometimes she seemed annoying, begging for money, asking to use a phone. Neighbors had long complained of her. One of them told a story of how Mary had been invited in to use the phone and then stolen something. Her thefts were commonplace. The addiction she suffered was expensive, sometimes up to five hundred dollars a day.

When I asked her what landed her/him back in prison, Mary said, "I was getting into a trick's car and this Hollywood movie just flashed in front of my eyes, and the next thing I knew I was just driving away in his car. When the police found me I had no idea where I was or whose car I was in!"

Mary's physical and psychiatric problems and track record meant that even the most sympathetic social workers and police and sex trade workers eventually tended to give up on trying to help her. Her roommate, also her boyfriend, had evicted her numerous times.

When she was in prison, which was frequent, she would keep us in touch with where she was. Our other source of information about the nature of her frequent disappearances was another transgendered person, Pauline.[1] Pauline is Mary's sponsor, her mentor in her twelve-step recovery, and, having successfully overcome an alcohol addiction of her own, was everything a sponsor should be — solicitous and concerned.

That Mary was among the city's most marginalized individuals was undeniable. Her presence was always painful, that of someone

---

1. Names are changed.

constantly in torture from internal as well as external adversaries. Even the homeless, even other crack addicts looked down upon her. Watching her was akin to watching a suicide in progress.

When she entered our church, like Del, she came to eat. This shocked me because most sex trade workers didn't have to rely on the church for food. If they came to our evening service or dinner it usually meant that their addiction was so out of control that every spare penny was going for drugs, or that they actually wanted to be there. Mary came because she was hungry and because her roommate had said it would be safe.

Del had already become a regular attender, and this also helped Mary feel more secure. I made sure that she was safe in all the ways that I could. I asked her to serve Communion, signifying to the other evening service congregants who treated her with ridicule that she was accepted and acceptable. This, I hoped, would help. I got her to help in the kitchen, introducing her to our community staff, who were happy to have help and didn't care what Mary looked like, and I spent time just listening to the stories of her life, stories of abuse, addiction, and ostracism.

Her background was poor, as contrasted with Del. She grew up on the prairies with alcoholism and sexual abuse from an early age in an extremely dysfunctional household. As soon as she could manage it she left home and moved east, becoming involved with the drug and street culture. The church had always been a place of menace and danger. Whenever she had ventured in, both pastors and congregants had laughed at her, snubbed her, condemned her, and of course, prayed for her.

The only reason she had entered our church was for the food. When she was invited into worship and noticed that queer others were also present, Mary said she felt welcomed for the first time in her life.

"You are definitely my Minister, and this is definitely my church!" she announced in a stoned voice the first time she attended worship. She said others in Toronto had fed her, but she never felt part of the congregation. They didn't like her transgender person or they didn't tolerate her addiction or they didn't like what she did for a living. She would look around and see middle-class faces at worship or condemning working-class faces, and she knew she didn't belong.

The level of her life of banishment from every possible institution or community was extreme. It was hard for me to imagine a place that would welcome Mary, in the paraphrased words of a hymn, "just as she was." Even the tolerance of the morning service would not have been tolerant enough. I suspected kids would laugh at her, or someone would make an inappropriate comment or she would simply look around the sanctuary and see no others who were queer enough.

At her graduation from the one chance at rehabilitation that she received, she thanked me and our community of faith even though I felt we had done very little other than exist there for her. In a sense the problem was and is that Mary continued to care what others thought of her and continued to care about others. The tragedy seemed heightened because of this. Many in the evening service suffered from some degree of brain damage or had been wounded so thoroughly that they lived in their own relatively impervious worlds. Mary was shy around others because others still had the power to hurt her. The grace of her evangelism to me and to our congregation was that she allowed us also to help her. "You visited me in prison. . . . No one else ever did."

Mary became a sort of test for us in an even more extreme way than Del. If Mary, who was accepted absolutely nowhere else, could make our congregation home, then anybody could. Or that, at least, was our hope. That she wanted to make our congregation home was an answered prayer. In her periods of sobriety, Mary added her opinions on liturgy, outreach, and pastoral care. Having been the victim of everyone's intolerance, she could not afford to be intolerant herself and had also learned to ignore stares, silences, and sniggers from others. She taught me about forgiveness.

She also taught us to risk for the sake of our understanding of the gospel's call. When a volunteer of an organization that rented some space from us was rude to Mary, I was forced to defend her. "Everyone who enters this church is a loved child of God. Mary is a member of our congregation. I don't ask you to give her anything, but you cannot be rude to her. Do you understand?"

I hate confrontations and recoiled from saying it, but I felt I had to. Mary's hurt expression made it necessary and overcame my cowardice. I hoped the volunteer was also enlightened by the exchange.

Mary challenged my understandings of feminism. A transgendered person was fired from a rape clinic for being biologically male, and I was appalled that many on the left in media defended the action. Before Mary and Del, I might not have reacted that way. Mary and Del gave flesh to Butler's theory. What was a woman anyway?

> Del: I don't see getting excited about defining what has become for me increasingly a line drawn in the sand.

> Mary: A woman is what I am. That is how I know that I am a woman.

If "woman" is defined by one's position in terms of held power, Del and Mary — particularly Mary — held none. If "woman" is defined by one's oppression, one's marginalization, Del and Mary shared that. One might even argue that with the addition of female hormones to their bodies, genetically they were female.

A United Church women's group comprising of younger women voted to extend membership to Del (and Mary too if s/he so wished, but Mary was never out of prison long enough to attend). Retreats for "women only" were redefined.

Even in a man's prison, Mary maintained her long styled hair, wore makeup, and tried her best to make the orange uniform look stylish. One can only imagine in nightmare form what life was like for her in there. One of Mary's principal concerns was that her real clothes, her women's clothes, be made available at her release. The act of bravery involved in simply dressing in women's clothes brought home to some of our biological women their perhaps smaller acts of bravery in wearing women's clothes.

Mary, unlike Del, was principally attracted to men. She shared this with all our gay male congregants, but because she was so obvious about this, it allowed them to feel more comfortable expressing their attractions in what was still a predominantly heterosexual congregation. "Straight" congregants could not avoid the "issue" when Mary was present. She made them aware, whether uncomfortably or comfortably, that this was a welcoming place for queers. They could "see" Del as male but they knew Mary was queer. One lesbian member said jokingly that with Mary around she felt "straight." With Mary around, she certainly was "straighter."

In a sense, Mary was the one who allowed all the others, no matter how queer in their own way, to feel for a moment normal. Even Del admitted that her trials were small in comparison. Though rarely actually present, Mary was often present in prayers. Everyone in the evening service and many in the morning service knew who she was and that she was in prison. Everyone also knew that Mary was a real member of our congregation.

She testified to her faith eloquently and wherever she found herself, particularly in prison where she had difficulty connecting with Christians. Her faith was hardly liberal, her Jesus was decidedly male, and her scriptural knowledge tended to literalism. She also loved the story of the Ethiopian's conversion, although not because Mary saw herself as the Ethiopian. No, she was the woman at the well. She was like Eve, like Esther. There was nothing strange about Mary's womanhood to Mary, just to the rest of the world.

Mary would have loved to come to Godtalk, our version of Bible study, but Mary was in prison or strung out on crack and mixed up her days and times. I tried to connect her with prison ministries, but she was always transferred before anything gelled. Mary's example reminded us how precious the opportunities for community were that we shared as Christians. She was a living reminder of our blessings, so often taken for granted.

A theology of hospitality was also tested when Mary was at her worst, when she was stoned or desperately needy or even possibly dangerous. Was she still welcome then? At the evening service it was a rare day when someone was not belligerent, or epileptic, or stoned, so yes, Mary was even welcome then. Even in the morning service, there was the occasional interruption of the "crazy" and the continual interruption of babies or children who didn't want to leave their parent's side.

There is no doubt that Mary's extreme variety of queerness tested and tried our attempts to be inclusive. It was a test I think we passed, with some degree of difficulty. I developed a style of worship leadership, along with others, that was far more free-form than our morning bulletin would suggest. In the evening when we had no bulletin, the liturgy was driven by the needs, wants, wishes, and interruptions, inspired and rude, of the congregation and the rituals which, although bended, were never broken.

Along with others, Mary and Del loved ritual, and had enough of a Roman Catholic background to find some "high liturgy" compelling. We lit candles for prayer purposes. We celebrated the Lord's Supper every Sunday. We moved into a Taizé-style worship with repeated chants and refrains, but we still had live and interactive exchanges. Everything centered on prayer, especially for Mary, because she was so often in our prayers or we in hers.

Prayer framed my prison visits with her and my street encounters. Prison visits mean hours of endless waiting, making the visitor feel in prison. "Outreach" felt like really "out" there outreach with Mary as its recipient. I waited for her to conclude anything about lifestyle changes, but never made any suggestions. It seemed to me that any changes in Mary's life were the work of the Holy Spirit anyway and not ours. Mary sought out and successfully finished rehabilitation for the first time in her life, only to relapse within a few months. Mary spoke of and occasionally managed to stay away from the street, but not long enough. Mary said that because of our hopes and prayers for her, she seemed to come to care about what happened to her body and soul more, but never enough. She said she felt loved by us. For us that was enough.

I said I felt loved by her. I did. I understood what it might look like in those brief glimpses of grace we receive, to feel loved by my very different, very queer neighbor. I was one of "them" to Mary. I was, without a doubt, the very image of a Pharisee to her when she first knew what I did for a living and where I did it. She found it in her heart to forgive me for standing in and with an institution that had only meant hatred for her. Del had taught me to check my judgmental instincts. With Mary, I practiced this newfound gift and discovered, like every skill, that it got easier with practice.

The presence of the queerest of the queer in our midst at Emmanuel Howard Park became the question to all of us as to how seriously we wanted to be Christian. When our members visited them, other congregations, especially suburban ones, often seemed like clubs or community centers by comparison. We, who supported the openness of our Communion and community, felt Mary's presence as a blessing.

She, by her very physical presence or by her supported physical absence, would never allow us to become too comfortable. And when she was absent, someone equally queer would always be a visible reminder of otherness.

Is she a sinner? Absolutely yes. Are we all sinners? Absolutely yes. Mary's presence reminded us of our sin to our discomfort. We, those less queer, reminded her of her sin to Mary's discomfort. The differences among us kept us uncomfortable, not more comfortable, and our commitment to a sinless Christ kept us repentant. The differences among us kept us faithful to the quest for hospitality as scripturally dictated and more faithful, we prayed, to a Christ who forgave sinners just like us when our hospitality failed.

Chapter Eight

The Queer Continuum

Creating a church that would allow everyone to gather around the table of Christ demanded of congregants a degree of what could be called "Christian formation" perhaps not required in more homogeneous congregations. Where doctrinal uniformity was not required, congruence around the biblical precept of hospitality was. What seemed to be necessary was an admission on behalf of everyone that they indeed shared some of the "queerness" of our more queer members. Those who saw themselves as absolutely "normal" had the most difficulty. The more humility in one's ownership of the church, the more comfortably one accommodated the strange new faces.

As older members became a smaller percentage of the church body, dress codes relaxed even in the morning service. Younger members dressed more casually as did, of necessity, evening service members. Suits and ties began to look strange, even on Sunday morning. For those who could not imagine attending a worship service except in a suit and tie, where suit and tie were beginning to appear "queer" (different, marginalized), queerness came as a new experience. Where elder members were used to seeing others like themselves and suddenly found themselves in a minority, queerness became a new experience.

This was often difficult to name or reconcile, as everyone wanted the church to grow numerically and knew that wasn't possible without, it was assumed, becoming welcoming toward young, more traditional families.

"I look around and don't see anyone I know!" one older member voiced to me. She felt alone at coffee hour after the morning service and afraid of the evening service people who would occasionally attend both services. Feeling vulnerable as an elderly female was justifiable and understandable. For the first time she was experiencing what it

114

felt like to be vulnerable at her own church. It was no longer quite as comfortable a pew.

The fact that the elderly were no longer feeling as comfortable in church was something we addressed in our monthly "Care of the Congregation" meeting. The question was how to rectify that without being less welcoming to all the ones most queer. We decided to have seniors' luncheons three times a year specifically to celebrate our seniors. Seniors who had not been seen in church for a while made an effort to attend those luncheons, which became a great success, with an average attendance of fifty to sixty.

We also addressed the issue (or pseudo issue) of transportation for those less able to make it to worship. Those with minivans were introduced to those who needed a ride (mainly seniors), and several were made to feel welcome in that way. One senior, who had been a single mother, was invited to our single mothers' weekly brunch, to share her experiences of now being a single grandmother. She enjoyed it so much that she stayed and took part in other more "youth"-oriented retreats, for she had developed cross-age ties successfully.

Developing such new friendships outside of one's comfort zone became a critical path for allowing comfort zones themselves to broaden. A refugee family, through conscious effort, became friends with a young Canadian family despite the language barrier. Everyone became familiar with the more visible queer members, at least enough to know that they were members. An older woman (who might be called a bag lady) came regularly to the morning service and seniors' lunches as well as Family Games Nights. If she was absent, she was missed.

As the young woman who started Family Games Night (an evening at the church with potluck dinners, board games, and babysitting provided) announced once from the pulpit, "Everyone here is a part of this 'family' so everyone is included." The word "family" had taken on an entirely different meaning.

We were not always successful. One particularly active and supportive family left audibly and publicly during a morning worship service. I had suggested that a tax rebate check sent out by the government to all tax-paying individuals might be donated back to the poorest among our congregation by giving it to the church. "I pay my fair share of

taxes. I shouldn't be made to feel guilty!" muttered the husband an-
grily as they left after the announcement. I called them immediately
and received the explanation that our church had become way too
left wing for him. That we remain hospitable to conservatives as well
as liberals was important to us, and I interpreted this as a personal
failure.

Upon reflection in a number of forums, all of us feeling their loss,
we concluded that the "presenting" issue was probably not what was
really operative. More realistically, they probably had felt the sting of
"queerness," looking around the congregation and not seeing themselves mirrored very frequently (suit/tie/well-dressed) in others. The
husband admitted to me that what he wanted was a church where he
could feel "comfortable." With our church, he was out of that comfort zone. He was beginning to feel queer. Nevertheless, we named a
room after them because of their faithful membership and generosity.
We felt their leaving as a loss and failure, which I believe it was. The
operative question for this grand experiment was how to allow people
enough comfort. This was much easier with those who had always felt
queer, those who had always been queer, than with those who had
never felt queer.

One of my favorite sermon themes was the radicality of being a
Christian in a nonworshiping world, for I believed that to be the
case. Feeling uncomfortable, feeling queer in church was, in a sense,
a discipling for just how queer one might feel as a Christian in the
outside world.

During an interview, I was asked about my radio show moniker,
"Radical Reverend"; "What's so radical about the radical reverend?"
and I answered, "Being Christian in a secular world." I believe that
was accurate. If the more middle-class among us felt strange/queer in
our church family, by being openly Christian at work and socially we
were also strange/queer. Our queerer members again experienced the
dissonance of their Christianity less because their lives were lives of
dissonance.

The example of queerness in our midst at church, their sharing of
experiences of exclusion, gave those not so obviously queer courage to
out themselves as Christian in the world. What had we to be afraid of?
After all, although being Christian was unfashionable, it didn't invite

the violence, the taunts, that transsexuality did. For Lent one year, I announced that I was giving up TV for forty days. The majority of the morning service understood this as a hardship. For many in the evening service who couldn't afford a TV, some of whom were homeless, it wasn't much of a "discipline." Their lived reality helped "us" live our resolves. What actions seemed queer to our unchurched friends and family became less queer in our church family.

Christian formation became a process, in part, of becoming queer (strange, different). Many commented on this when they would return from other church experiences. Many commented on the "cost" of being a Christian at our church. One member, a straight, white, middle-class male told me, "This church and your sermons and the people around me really make me squirm some days, but that's good. ... That pushes me into new directions."

Hospitality as operative theology also pushed me in new directions. As a left-leaning, traditionally United Church person, I was incorporating more and more Roman Catholic liturgical traditions because they were welcoming to many of our members with Roman Catholic history. As a feminist and budding queer theorist, evening service members taught me that my own political views were just that — my own political views. Many in the evening service were more conservative in all senses than our morning congregation. God as "He" wasn't "corrected." If someone wanted to take part reading scripture or voiced an opinion, hospitality became more important than inclusive language. Neither was "correct doctrine" or "correct liturgy" or, increasingly, "correct" anything. If we were to be truly welcoming, latitude in opinions about most things had to be present.

What emerged was a question of whether we were compromising our integrity. Our response tended to be that our integrity was our hospitality. And so, at one time or another, our sanctuary housed just about everybody, from Mormons to Marxists. Hospitality seemed to be the pastoral equivalent of theological nonjudgment. Thus, if it had indeed been my statements about tax rebates from the pulpit that upset the family that left, I would have refrained from making them, at least publicly. But upon reflection, the real issue seemed to be more about "hospitality."

So we did lose and might again lose members for whom hospital-ity was not as important. This, in a sense, was the outer edge of our own hospitality, the end of our own stated inclusiveness. We were and are committed to inclusiveness. If inclusiveness becomes impos-sible for some, they exclude themselves. If the sensation of queerness (strangeness/difference/marginalization) is too much to bear, then our congregation is not a good fit for those persons. We felt this process to be preaching and living the gospel as we understood it.

The continuum of queerness was something we all felt to some degree, or came to feel. We all came to feel at least somewhat queer. To feel queer became synonymous with feeling uncomfortable, which became synonymous with feeling and declaring one's Christianity.

This was nowhere more clear than when I presented the opening chapter of this book to a "Queer Studies Symposium" at a university. There were no apparent Christians or Christian content included in the three-day conference except for my piece, and I made sure to wear my collar just so that I could feel "queer" among the queers. There was not only incredible interest in what a Christian minister could possibly say about queer theory or queerness generally, but then also astounding support for what I said. Many have continued to e-mail me, and a few have even attended our worship. When the standard look was radical chic, a collar became the very symbol of queerness. Queers understood that. To be an "out" Christian at a queer studies symposium was queer indeed. It was also queer evangelism.

Beginning to Speak
to the Queer Continuum

Those who had been rejected by the world continued to arrive at our church's doorstep. Food became less and less of a draw. Sanctuary was the greater need. Community, family, acceptance, and love were required by the ones who came and stayed. After Del and Mary, they felt less queer and less judged. For other queers, the presence of the queer became invitational. Those congregants who were already part of the church relaxed, got real, let their own strangeness and craziness show. Here are some of their stories.

Colin

Colin was a young gay man, member of our congregation, and visitor to the church at least four times a week. The frequency of visits was because as a street person (although he did find housing within the first year) and artist and schizophrenic, he needed food, shelter, and spiritual support. When we had our directory produced, Colin was elated, because he could show his biological family what to him was his "real" family.

Colin looked like I imagine John the Baptist would have looked. He had long stringy hair, poor teeth, and thrown-together clothing, and was extremely thin. His body was diseased in a number of ways, and this manifested itself in a number of running sores visible on his hands and face. He was prone to ranting loudly at the street corner, and most of his ranting was about the end of the world as we knew it. Colin was intensely interested in weather patterns, hurricanes, earthquakes, and strange biological events such as mutating species. All of these were for him proof that the world as we knew it was coming to an end.

His prophesying always had a biblical cast. He would almost daily come in to my office to point out some piece of scripture that he believed contained an important message for the day. Because his Bibles were always getting lost or stolen, he routinely needed new ones. He would also give me his word of the day. This "word" was often funny, sardonic, mystic, poetic but never boring. Sometimes he would simply be angry and rude, and I would have to ask him to leave because during the day there were children present at a day school in our church. He would almost always be apologetic and realize that his disease was getting control of him.

Again, as one of the queerest among our congregation, Colin was used to a life of abuse and violence. He strained our patience, but we, committed to our hospitality mandate, learned how to live with him in a way that respected both his and our boundaries. It slowly dawned on me that although couched in ways that made them hard to hear, most of Colin's rantings were accurate. For instance, the world will indeed end unless we pay attention to our environment. Evil does lurk behind the most innocent facades. Peace and grace by way of Jesus

Christ are our only hope. But more to be noted than the content of his speech was the form. Cutting through the normal hustle and bustle of our street, the normalcy of the surroundings, was this queer figure speaking about God. It dawned on me that if John the Baptist were around today, he would be drugged and contained. Colin had escaped from those restraints, chemical and otherwise, and bravely maintained his right to prophesy.

I came to welcome the "word of today" from Colin. His "interruption" of my daily work, especially his interruption of my prayers, became a daily test of my own ability to be hospitable, our secretary's as well. The way we treated him became a sign to others who used the building — students of English, teachers, volunteers of various sorts — that we meant what we said about hospitality.

Gradually, through Colin we learned that far from being an interruption of our work in the church, Colin was our work in the church. He knew the church belonged to him, although he played the game of being polite and asked if he could use its facilities because it made us feel important when he asked permission. His work with us was critical because he was present not just on Sunday but all week long. All week long we had to "live" inclusiveness.

Catherine

With Del, Mary, and Colin at the outer edges of queerness in our congregation, everyone else existed on what I came to think of in this study as the "continuum of queerness." Catherine is a masculine-looking biological woman who happens to be lesbian. She is also the mother of three children and a partner to another member of our church. By trade, she is a chaplain whose work is carried out with ex-prisoners and those still in prisons. Welcoming her into our congregation and our morning service and her eventually becoming our Presbytery representative[1] seemed a dramatic first test of the congregation's ability to make her welcome.

Catherine's children also became valuable members of our confirmation class, and her son sang in the choir. She was a vocal and

---

1. Presbytery representative is that person who represents the congregation at the next church court — the presbytery.

funny member of council and influenced the work of a number of committees. When we considered going through a process of becoming an "Affirming"[2] congregation, her input caused us to forgo the process. She felt that she didn't want her involvement in the church to be "about" her lesbianism, that the process "outed" gays and lesbians and put their sexuality ahead of their commitment to Christ. We agreed.

Though a member of the morning congregation, Catherine sometimes attended the evening service. She had a good overview of the life and work of the congregation and the wider church through presbytery. Her presence in the pews and often in the choir was a visible reminder that inclusiveness was practiced both morning and evening. She was a wonderful "bridge" between the straights, who were feeling queerer by the minute, and the queers, who were feeling straighter by the minute. She was likewise a wonderful bridge between morning and evening experiences. "I felt really included and that the process here was fair. You didn't push your politics but kinda allowed people to become more embracing, more loving at their own speed. . . . I can feel comfortable here enough to worship without thinking of all that other shit."

Lesbian-headed families — of which at that time we had two, who both attended the morning service — allowed the straighter among us to see family in yet another new way. The children were just as together or not together as in more traditional families. More traditional families felt allowed to show their queerer sides. "The integration of queers and others has felt very natural," said Catherine. I asked Catherine what the word "queer" meant to her. She responded, "It's not enough to say 'on the margins.' There's a demonization that happens to those on the margins as well, a demonization that's difficult, if not impossible, not to internalize." Catherine pointed out that "straight" needed "queer" in order to feed their own sense of security. As in Foucault, homosexual was an invention that made heterosexual possible. "The easy answer is that we're one thing or another thing. The

---

2. The "Affirming" process in the United Church of Canada requires congregations to go through a period of meetings and discernment culminating, it is hoped, in a stated willingness to welcome an openly gay or lesbian as clergy (transgendered person is not included).

harder answer is that we create each other and ourselves. Rather than collapse everyone into the same, difference allows difference."

The more queer, the more queer, the more queers, the more queers. The greater latitude of behavior we allowed to coexist, in a sense, the greater the latitude of behavior we could allow ourselves before other judgment or self-judgment commenced. For Catherine, what did it mean to her to be female, or woman? "I remember hating being female when I was really young and wanting to have a sex change but that was only because boys got to do all the exciting stuff and it seemed to me like girls never got to do anything exciting. Having breasts sucked. It ruined my athletic career!"

When or why did that change for her? "I discovered there was this really cool thing women could do that men couldn't — have children! That made me more appreciative of my biology. And the times have changed."

Have her children changed her perspective?

I remember when my former partner allowed my son to put on make-up because he wanted to and thought it was fun. Then, of course, he went outside and had the crap kicked out of him by the other kids, because he looked like a drag queen. You can push the edges, but you got to be strong enough to be ready to have the crap kicked out of you if you do. My kids have had to have strength. So have we....

How about her Christianity?

I've often been accused of being a closet fundamentalist, and I guess at times I probably am. You can simplify a lot of our faith into simple statements of faith that just about everyone can understand. That's one of the strong points of evangelism, and it's something that as a chaplain I find really useful. You can answer the hard questions prisoners have about what happens after death, for example, which is really important because I've got a lot of guys who are grieving over someone they've killed. They need to know that's not the end of the story. Before, evangelizing was more about colonizing people; now I think it's having the courage to make strong statements and stand behind them.

What about Christian morality?

Unlike statements about what we believe, I don't think you can answer all questions as to "doing the right thing" with anything that's going to be right all the time. Queers can teach everyone how to faithfully involve yourself with the moment. We really have to be clear that the church has made some terrible mistakes doing just that. As Christians, we first have to repent.

Sandra

Sandra, a lesbian mother of one and about to be mother of a second child, just showed up one day in the morning service with her little boy and her partner. Again, her presence was an adjustment for some. She described a moment in service which had moved her. Her partner, Maureen, had instinctively put her arm out and around her. Sandra became aware that the new Albanian family that sat right behind her and had Muslim backgrounds might be shocked by this. She became self-conscious. I offered that after all the Albanian family had been through, a woman putting her arm around another woman wouldn't be comparable. I also explained that in our "Intro to Christianity" class, which this family had attended before becoming members, we very clearly went through what it meant to become a member of our congregation in terms of inclusiveness and in terms of the issues around sexual orientation.

Why had she chosen our church?

We had been attending M.C.C.[3] and that was fine, but for one thing it was pretty far away and, for another, it's one thing to be accepted into a community where you're already accepted and it's another to attend a place where that's not guaranteed. I felt I wanted to integrate into our immediate community. I used to go, before M.C.C., to a church that was very literalist in its approach. You couldn't smoke, you couldn't drink, you couldn't do anything...and it was hard for me being gay. I felt that this, a United Church, was a more accepting church and also because there was a female minister. I think that helped. And because we have Joey [their son] and we wanted to be able to put him into Sunday school.

Sandra spoke of the difference within her own family in terms of being marginalized and being accepted as a Christian and as lesbian.

---

3. Metropolitan Community Church is a congregation specifically for lesbigays and transgendered and is situated in downtown Toronto.

My father's a Presbyterian, and he asked me if I was praying (for my family's health) and I said I was, and he said well, I'd have to do something too if I expected God to do something for me — and that was of course, change my lifestyle. In order for God to answer my prayers, I would need to have a lifestyle change. In that church there's no way in a million years I'd ever come out. It's important for me to be able to be this comfortable in order to be here.

When Sandra and her partner Maureen signed Joey up in Sunday school, the teacher trying to fill out an attendance card asked the name of the father and was told, "Maureen." It took her a few minutes even though she was one of the older members, but she laughed and "got it." I asked Sandra if that experience had made her feel a little less welcome. "Not at all. We thought it was kind of funny. I think she [the Sunday school teacher] felt more embarrassed than we did."

What about God? Is God accepting?

I really felt like, when I was growing up gay, that God was a punishing God. That came out of that more rightist church experience and I think I still carry some of that, and I'd like to get away from that, to a more loving view of God. There are many books written in a sexist tone that have influenced me. I think where the Bible's concerned, I take what works and leave the rest behind. I've done some reading about translation and the history behind it all. I try to get versions of the Bible where the language is inclusive.

How has Jesus changed for you?

He's become a much more loving, forgiving kind of figure, whereas before he was so much more removed. I would question why gays and lesbians stay in more homophobic churches. I think it's a kind of internalized homophobia, internalized hatred. To live with a partner that you can't be upfront about in your church is just strange and sad.

Sandra became a member of our property committee. She was personally invited to do so by a middle-class male member. Unintentionally, just about every committee involved in church life had a queer on it. Because committee work necessitated getting to know one another a lot better than just sitting in the pews, this allowed the integration of difference to quicken.

How can we become a more welcoming church? "Put a rainbow symbol out the front of the church." I replied that I'd love to do just that but had had a hard time finding one. "Maureen will get one for you. There are so many gays and lesbians in the area, and that would make them feel welcome." And so, a rainbow sticker went up on our outside bulletin board publicly announcing that we were inclusive.

Since "like attracted like," the first members who were queer in any sense were the most difficult to integrate; but because we did, others came. The preaching and teaching that allowed one or two to be comfortable was, in a sense, more important than when many came. This was, of course, true for all visible minorities, including the blacks in our congregation.

Lillian

The presence of visible queers allowed those who felt queer but were not so visible about it to feel a greater degree of comfort in our sanctuary as well. Lillian is a straight, successful, university-educated young woman who grew up in a committed left-wing household where God, if thought about at all, was not central. She remembers going to church on her own as a little child because, as she said, "I've always felt the need for church."

I explained to Lillian that this study focused on the queerest members of our congregation, the transgendered; I also explained that in a sense she was part of the control group. "Wow, you mean I'm one of the normal ones? I've never felt or been one of the normal ones before."

Why did she come to our church?

A few years ago when my marriage was breaking up and I really felt the need for support and really knew nothing about the various denominations, I decided I'd go church shopping. I knew there were some churches that I wasn't interested in, for example, the Catholic Church or the Alliance Church. I just couldn't consider those because of my feminist principles. It's changed somewhat; I've attended Catholic mass with Pat's [her present husband's] parents and the message seems more open, but back then I really felt I couldn't step foot inside one without compromising myself. I wanted to pursue faith, not just fill a need of my own, to feel good, to feel superior. So that pretty well left the United Church or the Unitarian Church.

Why not the Unitarian Church?

> I felt I needed a challenge at that time in my life. I'd always thought
> about faith, but I'd never confronted it. The Unitarian Church was a
> really good experience, but I didn't feel that it confronted that issue; if
> anything it avoided that issue. It helped me avoid that issue. Then when
> Pat and I got involved, he was a complete nonbeliever who attended
> mass every Sunday to please his parents. Even though there were all
> sorts of things about his parents' church I couldn't accept, there was
> something about being with believers and about the faith. When Pat
> and I decided to get married we decided we wanted to be regular
> attenders of a church. We talked about church shopping. When we
> talked about the whole experience of church shopping itself . . . I mean
> his parents thought that it was blasphemous. You didn't go to a church
> just because it made you feel good. It was an obligation. But we felt our
> obligation was to find a church that was faithful but not oppressive.
> So we made a list of churches, and on criteria we decided on, drove
> around. We came here at Easter, that would be three years ago now,
> and knew we'd found it.

Why?

> It had everything that we were looking for here. We really felt comfort-
> able, we felt a spiritual presence here that was open to us, weird people.
> It was very joyous, full. I had no idea that the next week that there'd
> only be twenty or thirty people it seemed, although that didn't matter.
> I didn't go for Communion that day, although I felt that I could have,
> I a nonbaptized Christian. That was the very first time that I felt as if
> I could have. We were blown away by your sermon and how welcom-
> ing it was. I get emotional talking about it. My mother had made the
> decision not to baptize me because of how hurt she had been by her
> particular church. She had grown up in a very unwelcoming United
> Church. That day I just felt so welcomed. Everyone did.

Lillian and Pat enrolled their (his from a previous marriage) two children in Sunday school, became co-leaders of our "tween" youth group,
and were among the most active members in every way.

> We'd come occasionally to the evening service because of our sched-
> ules, and it was at the evening service that I first took Communion. It
> was incredible. We really felt we could belong here, even though we
> weren't married then. We were living together.

"How did you know that you weren't welcome at Communion at other
churches?"

Interestingly, the only time it was overt was at a United Church when I was a child. I was going to Sunday school, Canadian-Girls-in-Training, and there were many things I wasn't allowed to do because I wasn't baptized. It was a very homogenous congregation. And I think the fact that I went to church by myself bothered them. They didn't know quite what to do with me. They were nice. That I wasn't baptized kept coming up. Later — it was partly myself — I knew I shouldn't receive Communion under their restrictions, so I stopped. I wanted to respect their traditions. One time I went, a father and two kids got up to take Communion and the mother didn't. And there was something so sad in her look, so left out.

"Have you ever felt marginalized, queer?"

Yes. Pat's parents never really acknowledged me as his partner and, of course, I knew the rules of the other churches, but my marginalization seems so minor in relation to what some of our members go through, some others. You know, according to some other churches our marriage doesn't seem legitimate, and our children won't be either. To feel not worthy that way! But Pat's parents have said they'd walk by a gay man and not help him. They feel that's what their God requires of them, and they don't feel they've heard anything different from their pastor.

"How do you think of scripture, particularly perhaps those passages that might seem antiqueer?"

To be honest, I just don't, I guess that's honest. To me there's so many contradictory things in it I don't understand how people could take one passage in it. I don't think its contradiction is bad. I don't feel the need to reconcile it. I'm a writer, and some of it isn't very well written. Who knows what they really meant in some passages? I don't have a problem with all its facets.

David

David grew up in a rural community with a very homogeneous population and a very homogeneous church. He left it, in a sense, as a reaction against the conformity that he found everywhere. As a straight, white, middle-class male, with, as he said, "all the advantages," his rebellion was drinking, partying, suicidal behavior with an unfocused, unaware edge. "When I got married and we had Stephen [their toddler], everything changed. I had something to live for."

Always interested in history and particularly military history, David had majored in it at university and was seriously disappointed when he did not successfully defend his thesis. After the letdown, he seemed to bear up admirably and continued working at his job in a historical society and enjoying his role as main parent to Stephen. The fact that he was "Mr. Mom," as he described it, while his wife worked full-time, showed him how far he'd come since his youth.

For him as for others, one of the attractions of our church had been its welcoming atmosphere, particularly for children; he and his wife had attended the evening service, also for street people and other marginalized persons. Our church had even prompted thoughts of his own possible call to the ministry. "It grew out of my interest in history and particularly the history of the Protestant Reformation. God has always seemed a reality to me and nothing I've ever really seriously questioned."

Why this church?

> No doubt its closeness to where we live and the fact that we were in agreement with the United Church generally. I could never see myself being a part of the church where my wife was raised, its smells and bells. And she wasn't interested in going back there either. We knew we wanted Stephen to have the experience of church. I was impressed with the message that I heard very early on in our attendance here that everyone was welcome, and that meant gays, homeless, everyone.

David was involved with the committee work at the church as well, and their family came to Family Games Night. His wife had let an expletive slip while playing a game, something not usually heard in church. "Imagine a church where you could get away with that, where everyone just laughed. That would never have happened in either of our churches growing up."

I asked him if he had ever felt marginalized or queer in relation to church.

> I'm a white male; my home church was built by and for people just like me, but it's interesting. When I bring Stephen to the Moms and Tots drop-in group here, I'm the only male stay-at-home dad who comes out, and all the women look at me like I must be some kind of child molester! That's a new experience. I like the fact that I don't know

everyone and that there are some I might not even understand who are also members.

David was often seen working around the church during the week since he was one of a few stay-at-home persons who were able to offer some assistance when needed for building projects.

If there was ever anyone "normal" it should have been David, yet David also felt queer at times as more father than breadwinner and at a point in his own personal journey that involved soul searching and more questions than answers.

> We're your typical strained, overworked couple with a baby. I've come from and through some pretty dark places in my life in order to even be alive today. I'm lucky to be here.

The queer experience, the experience of being on the edge of acceptability if not wholly unacceptable, could even be extended then to the apparently most typical church member, a white, straight, married, psychiatrically normal male.

That being "queer" in relation to organized religion was a common feeling and state among our newer members and that the most queer — our transgendered members — were only that, the most queer, pointed to a continuum of queerness in our congregation and to questions about the continuum in regard to the question of Christian formation. What did our church mean by Christian formation?

Chapter Nine

Qu(e)erying Morality

Another Beginning

When I first arrived at the United Church as an adult, I thought I had come because I wanted my children to know the biblical stories so that they would understand Shakespeare. I also wanted them to have a forum for the transmission of values. Having no church background and raised as an atheist, I was attracted to a church that shared my values and that had recently decided not to deny ordination to someone purely on the basis of their active homosexuality. Having no church background myself, I was full of questions, including what "morality" this denomination stood for. I expected that I would have to lie, openly or covertly, about some aspect of my past, especially my sexual past, no matter how "liberal" the denomination seemed to be.

At this point, I would describe myself as having been called to that church. Those who are now called to our church, whatever their sexual histories, tend to come with all sorts of questions regarding the church's stands on various moral topics. The ones who are new to our denomination and church tend to come expecting to have to lie about some aspect of their past or present, especially their sexual past or present. One of the first areas of congregational life we try to address is that you don't have to lie to come to church.

They do not have to confess either. Neither did I. It astounded me and tends to astound them. If forgiveness is required, it is usually for churches in not welcoming newcomers. The confession of sin that takes place in the act of baptism is the realization of the Lordship of Christ over all aspects of our own lives (private and public) and the giving over of any private conceit as to our own Lordship. The forgiveness we have all received before confession, before baptism, before birth, through the cross is so overwhelming and so undeserved, what else could we say?

To the secular public (and most of the public is secular in that they do not go to church and do not consider themselves members), church stands for morality.[1] Church stands for tried-and-true codes of right and wrong, virtue and evil. Church stands for *truth*, as contrasted with the ambiguity of the cultural surroundings. Many are attracted by the firmness of this supposed foundation. Some are attracted by the promise of eternal life in a transient and mortal world. In contrast, one of the first lessons most people learn is that church itself is ambiguous, that even if the message from the pulpit is literalist and fundamentalist, the people in the pews and the stuff of their lives don't fit such frameworks. For those attracted to more inclusive denominations, like the United Church of Canada, it may feel as if there is no firm land left. This state has left some analysts blaming "liberalism" for the flight from the pews[2] and other analysts calling for more social justice and less emphasis on doctrine.[3]

There is no doubt that moral fervor exists on both ends of the theological spectrum. Whether social justice traditions with the emphasis on oppression and oppressed, or moral majority traditions with their emphasis on personal piety and personal sin, both strive for the "right" and against the "wrong."

> **Morality** n., pl. -ties 1. Moral quality or character; rightness or wrongness, as of an action. 2. A being in accord with the principles or standards of right conduct; virtue. 3. Principles of right and wrong in conduct; ethics.[4]

What is the basis for "moral" conduct codes for a Christian? Both sides of any debate inevitably seem to point to the biblical witness. For "conservatives" the exegesis is conducted in one way, of course, and for "liberals" in another. Witness Rudy's reading of the Sodom and Gomorrah passage in her fifth chapter.[5]

---

1. Reginald Bibby, *Fragmented Gods* (Toronto: Irwin, 1997).
2. E.g., "renewal" movements in the mainline traditions.
3. E.g., feminist and pro-gay/lesbian ordination movements in the mainline traditions.
4. *Webster's Unabridged Dictionary of the English Language* (New York: Portland House, 1989).
5. Kathy Rudy, *Sex and the Church* (Boston: Beacon, 1977). Rudy pulls out the principle of hospitality as the overriding moral imperative. Conservatives have in the past pointed to the sinfulness of homosexual behavior. Both point to another moral question: which one is right?

It is the very "rightness" or "wrongness" that has led to denomina-tional splits, death, war, all in the name of what is biblically "right" and thus "right" with God. Queer voices like the ones heard from Del and Mary or on the queer continuum, our own, are also sinful/human moral voices. Whether we read them colored with culture or the Holy Spirit depends on our own version of moral. But what if the Bible is morally ambiguous? " 'You shall love the Lord your God with all your heart, and with all your soul, and with all your mind.' This is the greatest and first commandment. And a second is like it: 'You shall love your neighbor as yourself.' On these two commandments hang all the law and the prophets" (Matt. 22:38–40).

This would seem to imply that all other possible commandments are lesser than these, that in particular, any extant moral codes should take a secondary position to these two commands. But what, if any-thing, has this "Great" commandment to do with morality or codes of rightness and wrongness? What does it actually mean to love God and your neighbor when it is used as a template for ethical or moral decision in any real-life circumstance?

For some clues, we again need to return to the biblical witness to examine how Jesus lived the great commandment, for scripture is nothing if not ambiguous as to what love for God and neighbor looks like in praxis.

Matthew

Loving your neighbor in Matthew begins by healing one's neighbor (4:23) through the power invoked in the Holy Spirit. Jesus says that certain among the neighbors are particularly blessed (perhaps deserv-ing of love?): the meek, the mourners, the poor or broken in spirit, the ones who are hungry for justice, the merciful, the pure in heart including the body, the peacemakers and the persecuted (because of righteousness, being as God wants one to be), or anyone who is reviled or persecuted because of faith in Christ (5:1–12).

Jesus announces himself as the fulfillment of the law. It is in his person that the law now resides. Yet he also announces a new and impossible fulfilling of the law, anyone who even, for example, looks at a woman lustfully is now an adulterer. We are to be as perfect as God (5:48).

All this acknowledgment of the impossibility of evading our own sinfulness builds to its logical climax. If we are all sinners, erring always as to the law and in God's eyes, we cannot possibly be in a position to judge others.

"Do not judge, or you too will be judged" (7:1). Again the operative point seems to be to humble Jesus' listeners, to assure them that there is not one of them more righteous than another. And the finale, "So in everything, do to others what you would have them do to you, for this sums up the law and the prophets" (7:12). Love your neighbors means doing to them what you would have them do to you. This is at least theoretically possible.

Those who follow Jesus need not follow the purity codes of the current religious powers. They need not bury their dead, only follow him (8:22). They need not fast (9:14–16). They can work on the Sabbath (12:1–8). They can ignore their biological mother and father (12:46–50). They can associate with the unclean and those, even women, of other nations (15:27–28). They do not really need to pay the temple tax (17:24–27). They cannot divorce even though the law of Moses permitted it (19:1–12).

It is faith that heals throughout Matthew's gospel, not deeds. Hospitality is demanded for the disciples, those sent. If hospitality is not found, the house is not worthy to stay in (10:11–14). A reference is made that backs up Rudy's exposition of Sodom and Gomorrah. Clearly Jesus sees the moral of that story as hospitality.

The disciples are promised chaos and persecution and hatred. Whoever acknowledges me is mine, says Jesus (10:32) — mentioning nothing about works or actions. Anyone who receives the one who claims faith in Jesus is receiving Jesus (10:40). Reward is promised for faith but clearly not in this life.

In the "Seven Woes" section of Matthew 23, the hierarchy of the temple is upended. The teachers are called to be servants and to take the loads off the backs of the people. Pointedly, no one on earth is to be called "father." In the Great Commission at the end of Matthew, the disciples are called to go and make other disciples, disciples of *all nations*, already a precursor to Pentecost and a further flouting of all purity codes. There is no command to test or catechize or accept some but not all. There is no description of the sort of person who would make an acceptable Christian, but instead a sweeping affirmation of all, implying all the world (28:19). The baptizing, the welcoming into Christian community precedes the teaching (28:20).

Mark

Mark's Jesus eats with tax collectors and sinners, the impure of all varieties (2:15). Again, the contravening of purity laws is among Jesus' first acts. Again, Jesus is not in the synagogue but outside it and his actions are hated from the beginning of his ministry by the rulers of temple life (2:24). This was presumably not because of his special powers but because of his immorality (breaking of the codes of rightness and wrongness) and his assumption of the religious authority of the rulers.

In chapter 7 of Mark, Jesus enters into a dispute with the Pharisees about what is unclean and what is clean. He delineates the difference between the commands of God and what he calls simply "traditions" (7:9). What he describes as tradition is the ritual washing done by observant Jews before eating. His actions would have seemed dirty, disgusting, and certainly unfaithful. Again, he holds faith and the ruminations of the heart/soul over and against any deeds or actions. " . . . nothing outside a person that by going in can defile, but the things that come out are what defile" (7:15).

"For truly I tell you, whoever gives you a cup of water to drink because you bear the name of Christ will by no means lose the reward" (9:41). "Whoever" again seems to mean what Christ says: whoever.

His comparison of faithful disciples to little children in Mark 10 seems to imply that acceptance into the kingdom, as Jesus called it, was reserved for those who held faith and had nothing to do with any accomplishment. Children in first-century Israel were not seen as pure and undefiled but part of the labor force of the extended household. They were seen more as untutored and savage adults needing strict guidance. They were seen as morally irresponsible.[6]

---

6. Perhaps the best argument for what little evidence remains of an ancient Jewish childhood is seen in Maimonides' extensive prescriptions for parenting in the Mishnah Torah.

Faith seems to have been measured by the approach to Jesus. Those like the woman who touched his robe believing in his ability to cure were cured and praised (5:31–34). It is in the approach, the following of Jesus, that faith is measured, rather than right doctrine or bravery or any deed at all, for the disciples are often castigated for their ignorance and blindness yet remain his chosen ones (8:27–37).

Children, the little ones, will enter the kingdom (9:36, 10:13–16) and those who become as "little ones," those who follow Jesus, who have not yet been instructed in any faith but simply want to be near him. Cited for special condemnation are the teachers of the law (12:38) as if the laws of moral conduct are a burden on the people. Prayers in faith will be answered, and forgiveness will be met with God's forgiveness (11:22–25).

As if in answer to those who would see the poor as the bearers of moral righteousness (as in some forms of liberation theology or liberalism), Jesus upholds the actions of the woman who anoints him with costly perfume. "The poor you will always have with you" (14:7). Again, our own logic as regards actions ethical, our own judgment would lead us astray — meaning away from his logic, his judgment.

Jesus knows that those around the table with him at the Last Supper will betray him and by his actions forgives them in advance. One might ask: if Peter and Judas were worthy of partaking in the Lord's Supper, who then, on the basis of their actions, should ever be kept away?

As he appears to the disciples postdeath, Jesus reiterates that belief is the only necessity for salvation and gives the signs of belief. They will speak a new language, be able to heal others, and will be impervious to poison (Mark 16:14–18). No mention is made of purity, rightness, or wrongness. In fact the actions of healing the sick and driving out demons, speaking a foreign language, and drinking poison would have been condemned as morally suspect by the temple authorities of the era.

Luke

All possible conventions of human-dictated morality continue to be questioned in Luke.

That an unwed virgin finds herself pregnant with Jesus heralds that morality itself is now answerable to God alone. No human code could anticipate such a rupture. No human code would have failed to condemn it.

Simon Peter displays another sign that seems biblically to connote faithfulness. He falls at Jesus' knees saying, "I am a sinful man" (5:8). Belief and faithfulness in action involves the recognition of Jesus as the Messiah and the simultaneous recognition of ourselves as in need of salvation.

"Woe to you when all speak well of you" (6:26). Loving your enemies and nonjudgment are again the hallmarks of the Christian life. In other words, the new morality, if we may call it that, espoused by Jesus is the opposite of any code, is the dashing of any rightness or wrongness scale. Justice condemns the unjust. Jesus loves the unjust. Virtue defeats the sinful. Jesus loves the sinful (all of us).

If we approach, if we recognize the source of salvation and ourselves in need of salvation, if we extend hospitality, then we are saved. The sinner's sins are forgiven (7:48–50). Nothing else is ever required. It is not difficult to see why such salvation is good news, salvation being life eternal in God's love, however we might interpret that.

The cost of this new way of life is obedience, an obedience that requires life itself, leaving everything behind (9:60–62). It requires seeing as our neighbor the one who is sent to us, the one we have been taught to see as unclean, the one we least expect, the Samaritan (10:25–37).

Lest we turn this into a new kind of "work," the parable of the Good Samaritan is followed by the Martha and Mary story. All that is required is that we sit at his feet and listen. We are not required to "do" anything (10:38–41). We have simply to ask for what we need from a heavenly parent who will always answer prayer (11:1–13).

Woe again to all those expert in the laws of morality! Woe to them for burdening the people and for being hypocrites, as if they too are not sinners (11:37–12:11)! The followers of Jesus can afford to be generous because they have already been given everything (12:22–34).

In Jesus' call to repentance, the call seems to be to repent of judgment of others, "Do you think that because these Galileans suffered in this way they were worse sinners than all other Galileans?" (13:2). It does not matter what they did if they did it in faith. Having faith is the approach, the hospitality, the repentance of ourselves, the answering of the call. The ones who come when invited to the banquet are the new righteous as well as they who do not look for repayment when they invite others to their banquet (14).

The prodigal son on the road is welcomed because he is on the road returning to the father. And he is welcomed while he is still a long way off. The prodigal has not said nor done anything, and yet the father runs to him and embraces him. He has simply approached, he has returned, he recognizes where salvation (saving grace) lies, and he has taken that road. It is a directional change. He heads back to the father because he has run out of options. To stay where he was, he would have died. His return is to save himself. This is all that is required (15:11–31). For him, good news indeed!

And in case we attempt to make a new morality, a new code of antimorality, we are reminded that the law is still the law and will always be the law (16:16–18). Whenever the human desire to solidify, to "monologize" as Derrida might name it, to usurp the economy of the gift, or to make static that which must be fluid, ethics or morality becomes a prison. Even as we try to make of fluidity a new standard, the standard evaporates. Jesus will not have us turn from him to ourselves. He and he alone *is* morality and ethicality. He is the law.

We will, of course, turn from him. Jesus understands the human need to set ourselves up as divine and to arbitrate issues of good and evil, wrong and right, but when we do we must repent and forgive, and then repent and forgive again (17:1–9). Long before Derrida and the whispering circle of chapter 2, we have a circle of forgiveness which has no human end.

The rich young ruler gets the most direct answer given: "No one is good except God alone" (18:19). Even as we think Jesus is giving a prescription, a set of rules for righteousness, the commandment is followed by, "Sell all that you own and distribute the money to the poor" (18:22), and we realize that there is yet more. There is always more.

The meaning of the prescription is simple: to be saved you must do the impossible, and it is a meaning instantly recognized by the crowd gathered. "Then who can be saved?" (18:26). Jesus clarifies again, "What is impossible with mortals is possible for God" (18:27). The disciples need reassurance and so tell the master that they have left everything for him. That is fine then; that is enough, Jesus says. You will inherit eternal life. We keep in mind that these are the men who will also betray him, deny him, and abandon him. Everything that you have to give is both enough and never enough morally and ethically.

As though to answer any misreadings of the story of the rich ruler, Zacchaeus, also rich, yet who gives only half of his money away to the poor and pays back four times what he has stolen, is granted salvation. Zacchaeus is forgiven, for he has extended hospitality and he has approached and named Jesus as Lord.

In case we think that giving money to the poor is taking shape as part of the new code, Luke's Jesus then renders unto Caesar what is, only a page later, Caesar's (20:20–26). Wealthy or poor, powerful or weak, enemy or friend; perhaps the new morality is a nonmorality that is contradictory, strange, and situation specific. But this is not a biblical version of situation ethics; this is always Christ's ethics. He is the one that does not change. He and he alone knows right from wrong.

Pilate and the Pharisees are the moral men in the gospels. Pilate pronounces moral judgment: "I find no basis for an accusation against this man" (23:4). He is the judiciary and speaks fairly as one. He washes his hands of the people's crime. It is important to note that even if Pilate had overturned the cry for crucifixion, this would have gained him nothing. The will of God would still have been enacted. Before God, the only answer is obedience. Jesus was obedient even to death on the cross. It was both justice and injustice in one act. It was both immoral and moral. It was unavoidable. It was both ethical and unethical. In the light of Good Friday, the distinctions of humans dissolve. We call it Good Friday for a reason.

We are forgiven because Christ is forgiveness. We are all found both guilty and absolved at the same moment. It is impossible for the moral and ethical paradox of the cross to be resolved by us. It can only be resolved by God.

When Jesus says, "The Son of Man must be handed over to sinners and be crucified and on the third day rise again" (24:7), he is speaking about us. *We are the sinful ones. We Christians* are the sinful ones. We are also the ones forgiven by the same act.

The risen Christ tells the disciples to preach repentance and forgiveness of sins to all nations. Their role is to be witnesses. Our role is to be witnesses.

John

John's gospel places moral decision cosmologically in a realm outside of human understanding and judgment. Perhaps more than the synoptics, John's clarion call is to relinquish any thought of a creaturely role in morality.

In the opening chapter of John, we have it stated, "But to all who received him, who believed in his name, he gave the power to become children of God, who were born not of blood or of the will of the flesh or of the will of man but of God" (John 1:13).

We learn that Jesus is the one who takes away the sin of the world. What does that mean? Does that really mean what it says? Does it mean that Jesus, in his death and resurrection, actually takes away human sin — that is, mine and yours? Does that possibly mean that everyone who believes in Christ has their own *moral* sin erased? Is this then not John's clarion call for the end of morality?

God sent God's son into the world not to condemn but to save all who believe in him (3:17). We learn that we can only receive what comes from heaven (3:27). As though testing this, one of the first to believe is a Samaritan woman who has, Jesus knows, been not only beyond the purity code of the Jews but also has "sinned" by having many husbands or lovers (4:1–26). Her belief spreads among other Samaritans. Those who have never been included because of the morality of their day are included because of their belief.

As in the other gospels, laws of right conduct are broken continuously. The temple hierarchy referred to as the "Jews" in John's gospel are always seen as the righteous ones, the upholders of correct and befitting moral conduct. It is praise from God that counts, not praise from men (5:44). All that matters, the work of God, is to believe in the one sent, that is, Jesus (6:29).

Another critical passage tells us that no one comes to Jesus except one who is drawn there by God, so that even belief is a gift of grace (6:45) and has nothing whatsoever to do with our efforts, our personal actions. It is no wonder, then as now, that nobody could accept it (6:60)! "It is the Spirit that gives life; the flesh is useless" (6:63). It is interesting that Jesus' detractors questioned his own right to authority based on where he was from, on who he was. "Surely the Messiah does not come from Galilee, does he?" (7:41).

Let us listen again to the line that says perhaps more directly than any other in the New Testament where Jesus Christ stands on moral judgment: "Let anyone among you who is without sin be the first to throw a stone at her" (8:7). I remember thinking that this meant the sinful crowd who would stone a woman to death for any reason. Perhaps we think that there is some difference between us and those people? Yet this is far more likely to be a reference to all of human moral judgment. But it is not just a statement about human moral judgment, but about God's. "Neither do I condemn you" (8:11). The ones who are sinful and the One without sin stand in front of the accused and neither condemns. Jesus counsels with the parting words, "Go your way, and from now on do not sin again" (8:11). Is this a proscription as it is so often interpreted, or is it a statement about the rest of the woman's life who now, more than anyone else probably, believed in the Messiahship of this One? For she would certainly now believe.

"If the Son sets you free you will be free indeed" (8:36). John's Jesus, who is absolutely divine, whose ancestry is one with creation, one with the Word that is God, this Jesus sets us free. Free from what? Says John's gospel, most assuredly free from sin and from judgment. No wonder the temple believed him to be demon possessed!

We can imagine updating their horror. We can imagine asking if that means that because we are Christian we are above all human-made laws. Yes, but also subject to all, and those who enforce it, our neighbors, never on a morally higher ground. Never able to judge the judges. Does it mean that we are no longer subject to any moral or judicial human judgment, as well, of course, as being "slave to all," servant to our neighbor? It is no wonder that Jesus' words have been preached on as if he is saying exactly the opposite, as if he were saying that unless we obey a set of "moral" principles we will be condemned. Christ, the undecipherable, leaves us with an ethics of ambiguity, an ethics of movement and moments.

The blind man who sees is not guilty of sin, nor are his parents. He is simply another witness to Jesus Christ (9:1–34). He is a witness whom the religious authorities ignore. The blind man is a witness because he was called by God to be one, not because of any good or bad conduct of his own. The true blind, the spiritually blind, are those who claim that they understand anything more than that Christ heals who he will when he will and calls who he will when he will (9:35–41).

We are sheep. Is there such a thing as a moral or immoral ewe? There is simply, John writes, the sheep who know the sound of their master's voice (10:1–21). The religious authorities reacted to Jesus as if he were a lunatic. As they still would. It is not Jesus' miracles that the sheep will understand as though it were Jesus' acts that should accomplish anything, but it is his very person who calls us. He, in turn, is God's lamb, who obedient also knows the sounds of *his* God, his master's voice.

"I came not to judge the world, but to save the world" (12:47). So often is the message repeated that we cannot help but hear (we who have ears). Why do we continue to judge each other with such zeal? Not that there is not judgment but it is always and only of unbelief, never of actions, never of a moral nature. Why does this message not bring the peace that Christ intended? Why does it make us so extraordinarily uncomfortable?

Sin and Ethicality

An immediate cry goes up from the religious authorities in response to Jesus' teachings for a reason. If the temple does not stand for an enforceable moral code, if you do not have to obey the temple to gain salvation, what happens to the temple?

We are the branches of the vine. We will bear fruit if we remain in Christ. Apart from Christ we can do nothing (John 15:5–8). If we obey Christ, everything will be given us that we need. If we obey the commands, which are the visible manifestation of invisible belief, that is, loving God and neighbor, we need not worry or fear at all. We are the chosen ones, we who obey. We will bear fruit, because we are now friends and branches of Christ. We are Christ's apostles but always also sinners (John 15:9–17).

How will we know that we are on the right path? We will undoubtedly be hated for it (John 15:18–19). "They will put you out of the synagogues; indeed, an hour is coming when those who kill you will think that by doing so they are offering worship to God" (John 16:2). The Spirit of truth, the Counselor will come and will guide us, despite the world's hostility. And our sorrow will turn to rejoicing. Again, we may have peace, for Christ has overcome the world (John 16:5–33). And so shall we.

We are the church, we who believe. How do we know who we are? We love one another. And what does that look like? In the stories about Jesus, it looks like nonjudgment, it looks like hospitality, it looks like outreach to the marginalized. It does not look like morality. Sin is inseparable from the law, both in the binary sense of opposites being necessary one to the other and in the biblical sense of sin and the law being born with the Fall. With Christ we are freed from sin, and as branches of his vine we are the new law *if* we reside in him. How do we know that we reside in him? We profess our belief and we love one another. A new kind of economy of the gift. A new sort of justice. All of it incarnate in one flesh and one body, Christ's.

This is a profound and radical sense of ethicality. It is as upsetting today as two thousand years ago. We feel set free because of it and yet, without rules, we feel like birds dropped from nests. If no human or church is our Lord, faith is all we have left. Moreover, what does it mean when we must make all those moment-to-moment ethical decisions of our lives? How will we ever know what we must do?

Tradition, the teachings of the Christian community, could mean the upholding of the very questioning that is at the center of the stories of Jesus, the maintaining of the fluid, living water, to use a scriptural term. It could mean a guarding against the tendency all creatures have to build walls with morals and codes against the other. It could mean rather than setting aside ourselves as "holier than," setting ourselves aside as more aware of our own sinfulness. Tradition could mean holding fast to the ethic of hospitality.

The promise of John 15 and 16 is also that we will never have to make ethical decisions alone but that the Holy Spirit will be with us always. How will we know it is the Holy Spirit and not some other spirit? Because Christ promises us we will not be left without him. How do we know that it is Christ who promises this? Because the Bible tells us so. In the beginning was the Word and the word.

Are there any guarantees? One could say absolutely yes and no. As Paul's writings attest, there are a thousand little and great disputes that plague the Christian community and individual Christians, and judgment always shadows all of them. Trying to love one another, we will, over and over, hate each other. And we will always be called back, as the temple was, by someone at the door.

Does this mean "anything goes"? Steven Seidman, a queer theorist, defines queer ethical theory as follows: "In challenging sexual object choice . . . queer theory suggests the possibility of legitimating desires other than gender preference as grounds for constructing alternative identities, communities, and politics."[7]

That there is nothing "normal" in the sexual arena (or perhaps any other) has been attested to by queer theorists since Michel Foucault, or that normal needs an abnormal to know itself. For Christians, the problem comes with individualism and modernist notions of "freedom." The Bible seems to say that morality, whether righteous or in rebellion against righteousness, is inevitably of the world. Christ's ethicality, if we may call it that, is absolute. The stories outlining Jesus' ethics always point back to Jesus who gives the commands. Any other standard or code may be contra Christ. Even where convergences fall, they are coincidence. There is only one way, and it is as narrow as Jesus Christ.

Insofar as communities are simply "alternative" as Seidman describes, they are no different from communities that are status quo. Biblically, whether we sleep with our husband or everyone else's, we are "in sin" apart from Christ. What our sexuality looks like, in Christ, is the work of the Holy Spirit through us. It presumably therefore is loving, hospitable, and draws us into community. Rudy makes the point that by those ethical parameters, nonmonogamy is closer to the

---

7. Stephen Seidman, "Identity and Politics in a 'Postmodern' Gay Culture," cited in Kathy Rudy, *Sex and the Church* (Boston: Beacon, 1997), 124.

mark. The problem with her logic, perhaps, is that as soon as *any* be-havior becomes prescriptive, it becomes moral. As soon as it becomes "moral," it is no longer obedient to Christ.

I struggled with this because I wanted answers. I struggled with this because I was taught to want answers in the area of morality as well as everything else. The radicality of New Testament ethicality is that with the coming of Christ into the world, the world loses its dominion over us and Christians are governed elsewhere. If "queerness" solidifies into yet another code of being, another morality, it too will be qu(e)eried. The "aliveness," the incarnate reality of Emmanuel is a promise that the guide will be ever present.

In other words, it might very well mean, anything goes as long as it goes after Christ. Like those who have been imprisoned for a long, long time, we also do not know what to do when we emerge into the light of freedom. Everything is new. Born again, this time of the Spirit, we, like the first Adam, have to name things for the first time. I cannot fail, because I have prior forgiveness and I will fail, because I am human and I *will* not be obedient. I will fail to discern the call of Christ in any life situation. But, like the prodigal son, I pray that my direction, at least, is accurate.

As lesbigay and transgendered liberation gives way to the challenge of queerness in this generation, we see that liberation shows the signs of sedimentation. As Del noted, "I don't fit in anywhere."[8] The Chris-tian response to Del is surely, "Yes you do, you fit in here." This is the difference between the radicality of the world and the radical-ity of Christian community. Liberalism says to the conservative, "We will not tolerate you here," but the Christian response says, "Yes you do. You fit in here." Conservatives may say to liberals, "We will not tolerate you here," but the Christian response says, "Yes we will."

Neither/Nor

Neither conservative nor liberal. As others attempt to solidify Christ's teachings into code, he always evades, slips away, shocks, changes. He brushes off rich and poor when either of them love their "rightness"

---

8. Conversation with the author, January 10, 2001.

more than him. He breaks purity codes but comes to uphold the law. He recognizes no earthly authority but renders unto Caesar what is Caesar's. He is perfect and stands corrected by a woman of lower caste and impure status; "even the dogs under the table eat the children's crumbs" (Mark 7:28).

Far from simply undecidable, far from deconstructionist, however, he promises the Spirit as our guide. He will always be with us. Far from moral, we are given only the most general of clues as to how to discern whether our behavior is in keeping with our guide.

We are gathered into community, but the community and its accumulated wisdom is always under challenge from the prophet at the door. Whenever the community, the church, becomes sedimented, whenever it becomes a moral arbiter, the knock at the door comes from the one excluded.

Even those who hate are welcomed at the table. But biblical witness shows that they tend to exclude themselves. They would not want to share food with the queer. Its visible corollary are the ones who come to the evening service but do not want to take Communion from a bag lady or eat from a plate of bread that has been touched by someone unwashed.

Revulsion and disgust are the reaction of the temple authorities to Christ and Christians. We might ask ourselves who inspires our disgust in order to find the prophetic voice. We might, in New Testament fashion, want to specifically invite to the table those who disgust us. Inclusion is only truly inclusive if the ones we hate the most are also at the table. Perhaps there is no Christian who does not struggle with this.

Inclusion also extends itself to the biblical witness. Because of its undecidability, we must always be open to another reading, another voice, another witness. The knock at the door might be not just a prophet but Christ himself. Scripture might come to correct scripture; indeed we are promised by Christ that it will. Jesus Christ will come again, we repeat in the Eucharistic prayer. The proximate witness might give way to truth at any moment. Unlike the deconstructive move, the movement of faith allows for the possibility of an answer. The answer might come. It would be its second coming.

Heteronormativity is not normative, neither is homosexuality nor any variation. Purity codes are all defunct, as are any attempts to live without any codes on the basis of a higher purity or on any basis whatsoever. Seeing ourselves as sinless or seeing others as sinners, feeling guilty or claiming innocence are all lack of freedom. Judgment or the conceit that we might live without judgment still is chained in binaries, chained in sin. If to be ethical is to live as Christ calls us to live, then that is as solid as Christian community can be. There is nothing firmer than that. There is nothing freer than that. Yet the attempt to nail answers down that would relieve us of our freedom, relieve us of our sin, is akin to the nailing of Christ to the cross. It will not hold him.

Queers can remind us of what biblically we should know. We should know that we do not know the answers, only who *is* the answer, to any of life's myriad ethical dilemmas. Instead, churches have replicated the temple and set themselves up as moral arbiters. Whether liberals denouncing conservatives or conservatives denouncing liberals, codes are erected as fortifications against the possibility of loving our neighbors. Whenever we, at church, think we really know what hospitality looks like, someone will come along and question that, just as did the couple that left at our own church.

Or another Del or Mary will come knocking at the door. If we listen to their message, we have a chance. Their message is *not that they are right*, and it is not that we are wrong. It is to be included at the table. Not just the soup kitchen table, but the table where we together share the Eucharist (thanksgiving).

Perhaps the process of qu(e)erying is the prophetic process? Perhaps it is another form of exegesis that needs to become the ongoing work of the church? Truth claims need to be shown as the slippery fears that they might be. In scripture there is only one truth, the truth that walked among us as Jesus Christ. In a sense the process of deconstruction is the closest the secular has come to that. Because deconstruction pushes at the weakness of truths as they vainly attempt to bolster themselves against suspicion, it has pointed some Christians back to their own text in a more faithful way. Queer theory has pointed some Christians to a more faithful understanding of evangelism, conversion, and church itself.

Either/Or

What then does one do? How then does one act? From where do we receive direction? "Hate the sin but love the sinner" is not biblical. It is a quote from Mahatma Gandhi.[9]

Christian churches sometimes act as if Gandhi's words were the great commandment, as if the sinner can be separated from sin, as if it were possible to be free from sin. Jesus specifically indicted such thinking when he both condemned and freed with the Sermon on the Mount: "You have heard that it was said, 'You shall not commit adultery.' But I say to you that everyone who looks at a woman with lust has already committed adultery with her in his heart" (Matt. 5:27–28). According to this, if a person has homosexual desire, he/she is guilty of homosexuality. Celibacy won't save you. Nonaction is not salvation. You are still the sinner. You are still under condemnation *except* that you believe in Christ. We are all racist, homophobic or heterophobic, sexist, condemned. And we are all saved with Christ.

Any of the great moral debates of the church when viewed queerly and biblically seem to speak from the world. Abortion and anti-abortion are both moral stances. Ordaining homosexuals or not ordaining homosexuals are both moral stances. The better question might be, are the abortionists and the antiabortionists invited to the table? Are lesbigays and homophobes invited to the table?

Does this mean that one never takes a stand against or for anything? It would seem that one takes stands as directed by the overwhelming directive, the great commandment, and the ethic of hospitality, or as directed by the Spirit. One is directed by the Spirit always. The Spirit will always direct us to love our enemies like ourselves, however. The movement is dissemination outward, to include, and inward, to be included, just as Christ gathered, upheld, and sent forth.

Del and Mary were hated ones with no home. Hated on the left because they didn't fit with gay or lesbian, hated on the right because they didn't fit with straights. In a sense, the only home they had or have is with Christ. This should mean with the church but most often does not. There are subtle and overt ways of excluding. There is the overt way of condemnation. "You are a sinner because you are

---

9. *www.nagpuronline.com/momgbook/*.

straight, lesbigay, transgender, and I am not because I am straight, gay, transgender." This manifests itself in teaching and preaching.

The more subtle mode is to represent only one segment of the population. Del and Mary walk into the sanctuary and see only men and women with children, couples, or straight singles. Everyone looks well dressed. Heads turn as they sit down. Or they walk in and lesbians sit with lesbians, gays with gays, nobody looks like them. Heads turn as they sit down. Or everyone is white or everyone is black or everyone looks and dresses as if they have a "real" job. Or everyone dresses casually, making them feel overdressed. Del's and Mary's presence is then met with scorn or, more likely, attempts to convert, the measure of which would be that Del and Mary would look more like them, whoever they are.

Can we be, as Paul says he tried to be, all things to all people? No more perhaps than we can be like Christ. But in the power of the Holy Spirit, we can be branches of that vine. We can *try* to be all things to all people. We can *try* not to foreclose the conversation. We can assume that the message will walk into the sanctuary rather than be found in the sanctuary.

Conservatives have claimed that all possible answers can be found in scripture. I have never, in this study, argued with that viewpoint. Rather, I have returned to scripture time and again to read it "otherwise." I have found nothing "moral" there. Liberals have claimed that we must be inclusive and not discriminate on the basis of sexual preference. I have agreed but not because of modernist notions of freedom and individualism but because of biblical precepts of hospitality and obedience to Christ and Christ's teachings.

Conservatives have claimed that you should love the sinner and hate the sin, and sin is almost always personal. I have tried to argue that if you hate the sin, you inevitably end up hating the sinner because they are inseparable in Jesus' teaching. Morality is another form of works righteousness. Liberals have claimed that "we" must accept "them." I have tried to argue that "their" claim is prior to ours biblically. And the biblical claim is prior to us all.

Conservatives have tried to argue against liberals and liberals against conservatives. I hope this study points to the necessity for both to love each other not just in words but by surrounding the same table, the table of Christ.

Poststructuralism and queer theory have argued against truth, and some Christians have argued against poststructuralism and queer theory, usually seeing them as relativists. I hope this study begins to show that both are arguing in the same direction but for different reasons: Christians out of obedience and poststructuralists and queer theorists out of a deep ethicality which is seen as an a priori call from the other. Again, both are called around the table. Queer theorists and poststructuralists may walk into the church.

Yet ultimately Christianity is critical of all things philosophic. Even the possibility of truth is left possible. Christianity is as queer as it gets. The Christian Church is the fitting home of Del and Mary, yet it takes Del and Mary to carry that message to the church. Can the church listen?

Stumbling toward Bethlehem, as it were, the evening service at our church tried to listen. Let us examine the process.

Chapter Ten

Qu(e)erying Christian Discipline

The Beginning of the Christian

There is no doubt that much was asked of early Christians, usually culminating with their very lives. There was also much asked of how they lived their lives. A professor asked me if our experience of church wasn't a sort of "foyer ministry."[1] By that he meant that little was asked of the participants except that they participate, and that the challenge might be the task of Christian formation. Or to return to Stephen Neill, to develop a high-demand, martyred church.

His question left me wondering and thinking about the whole matter of formation. Is this a system of developing what could be called "moral" behavior in the members of a church, or is it another set of demands that we make upon one another?

It struck me from my interviews but also from our experiences that a great deal was, in fact, demanded of those who became regular members of our church, and it had to do with their behavior, but not their "moral" behavior in the sense that made us (whoever we might be) more Christian than they (whoever they might be).

The process of formation became one of (1) truth telling and confession and (2) assurance followed by (3) evangelism and hospitality — all based on increased study of scripture (our proximate witness to Christ) and prayer.

Truth Telling

"Truth telling" from our experience meant that our church seemed to provide a forum, either one on one or in a small group (no matter

---

1. Professor David Reed, conversation with the author, February 2000.

what the stated point of the small group was), to be able to tell the truth. From the interviewed and lived experience, this usually meant telling the truth, usually for the first time in church, about the real content of their lives. Again, in our experience this often meant about those instances in which they had been or felt "queer." It almost always involved instances where they had been judged by others and certainly felt that they would or had been judged by church.

The reason this hadn't happened for them before in another church is that they felt, whether accurately or inaccurately, that they *would* be judged for their actions or who they believed they were. Inevitably the question they intuited had to do with an (as I've hoped to begin to demonstrate) unbiblical notion of sin practiced by churches. Our educational task was to point out the unbiblical nature of that personalized definition of sin and to repent as church for having propagated it.

So this step of Christian formation in our community did take the route of confession and repentance. The confession was theirs *and* ours, however, and the repentance was *ours*. Not that their repentance was not also part of Christian formation. A continuous repentance was necessary around all of our tendencies to be inhospitable or noninclusive. This was not just the newcomers' task but also the ongoing work of the congregation. I was guilty of this, when the couple mentioned in chapter 7 left. They, perhaps, were guilty of it as well.

Assurance

The truth telling or confession aspect of Christian formation as experienced in our congregation was then followed by a process of assurance. The assurance was that they were loved by Christ. This assurance was made manifest over and over again in and by the community. One congregant routinely asked me and any others she saw as possessing power, "Do you love me?" She was not alone in asking. I was not alone in being asked. The power of saying, "Yes," and living it out, we hoped, provided assurance, an assurance that came from Christ.

It was also followed by our repentance, as church, for leading them to believe that they were not worthy of God's love, that Christ had not died for them, and certainly, that they would not be welcome in a congregation of Christians. Or that they would be welcomed if and only if they lied about some aspect of their behavior. Or that if and only if they changed some important aspect of who they were, usually their sexuality.

By welcomed, we meant welcomed at the table of Christ and welcomed as they were. Not welcomed with an eye to changing them or reforming them, but with an eye to reforming our church if they could not feel a degree of comfort and safety there. To allow comfort did not mean to make comfortable. It meant, in practice, spreading the discomfort of being Christian around a little more equitably. Discomfort would not just be felt by queers, or the queerest of the queer, the transgendered. Transgendered congregants were, then, like the proverbial canary in the coal mine, the sign that all was healthy or not healthy in our congregational life.

If the transgendered could be open and accepted and made to feel and, really, to become part of our family, then all was well. If they, the most marginalized members, did not feel safe, then something was amiss. We were not living up to our Christian goal of hospitality well enough or humbling ourselves enough. The edge of safety was always shifting, and prayer and discernment were necessary to see where that edge lay.

Hospitality

Hospitality began to look like the process of evangelism as lived *from the inside out*. Both church and newcomer having confessed, repentance consisted of extending the same "love" to others. This presented an ongoing series of challenges for all on the queer continuum. We were always found wanting but always wanting to, as I would describe it, follow Christ, in this regard.

The reality of our basic failure was the very divide between morning and evening service. Even though there was drift between the attendance for the two groups, it was still obvious to the eye that there was a difference. Morning service people tended to hold jobs; evening service people didn't (at least the sort that paid enough to keep you off welfare). Even though there was huge variety in those two groups, like still tended to find like.

Our sinfulness or our reality before us in full view, we still lived the attempt to form alliances across that divide. The divide made us all aware at the very least that there *was* a divide and that our work as church was to love each other across it. That divide, as metaphor for all the other divides between us — very queer to not so queer, for example — kept the question of Christian discipline forever open. We were never truly disciplined or discipled, but always en route, always in need of formation, whether longtime member or newcomer.

This required ongoing educational work, from the pulpit and to the pulpit. That the question of Christian discipline pointedly did not often have to do with our sexual lives as a community did not mean that the issue was beyond our scope, or didn't matter, just that as in other "moral" areas God was the judge, not us.

Prayer

We taught each other how to pray and to pray often. Since what to do in the ethical questions of our moment-to-moment lives was neither easy nor made easier by scripture, prayer became the only answer. Rather than praying for specific lifestyle changes, because that was the "moral code," we were forced to pray for guidance and leave the direction up to God. Trying to live the radical freedom that was our Christian warrant required and indeed demanded the servanthood of prayer. If human judgment was not the final arbiter, whether that looked like church or conscience, then we really did need to engage with God on a regular and structured basis. Not that prayer then became a humanly imposed rule, but that it became a Christian necessity.

I preached on prayer often. Prayer dominated our meetings. Answered prayers were celebrated. Prayers for answers were upheld. Prayer and meditation became the skills that needed developing most. This, we experienced, also led to healing. If the limit of prayer is what God can do, prayer became the answer to almost every question for those among us (all of us) who longed for answers.

That the answers to our prayers were often deeply different and personal made the discipline of prayer biblical. Jesus Christ had promised not to leave us alone but to leave with us the Holy Spirit as comfort and guide. The promise, in our practice, was not betrayed.

"How else would we know what to do?" Mary commented from behind the plate glass of the prison.

Christian formation, I concluded, was very much a part of the process of our church. Individual lives were changed, but the great difference, perhaps, was that Christian formation was and is seen as something that the church does not impose on its members but that church and member are called to by Christ. The church is not seen as *formed*. The newcomer is not seen as *unformed*. Both are seen as in need of formation. If anything, the prophet being at the door, the church is the one called always to repentance and re-formation.

The concomitant call with hospitality to the church was and is humility. One thinks of the growing humility (in the face of many newcomers) Paul evidenced. From the opening to Romans: "Paul, servant of Jesus Christ, called to be an apostle, set apart for the gospel of God" (Rom. 1:1). He appeals on the basis of his service rather than leadership.

Romans

Paul, in his servitude, seems upon first reading to be, by a circuitous theological route, bringing his readers under sway of morality in the opening chapters of Romans, until we read in chapter 7:

> For I do not do the good I want, but the evil I do not want is what I do. Now if I do what I do not want, it is no longer I that do it, but sin that dwells within me. So I find it to be a law that when I want to do what is good, evil lies close at hand. For I delight in the law of God in my inmost self, but I see in my members another law at war with the law of my mind, making me captive to the law of sin that dwells in my members. Wretched man that I am! Who will rescue me from this body of death? Thanks be to God through Jesus Christ our Lord! So then, with my mind I am a slave to the law of God, but with my flesh I am a slave to the law of sin. There is therefore now no condemnation for those who are in Christ Jesus. For the law of the Spirit of life in Christ Jesus has set you free from the law of sin and of death. (Rom. 7:19–8:2)

Our response is one of gratitude, lived for the grace that we have received, whatever degree of queer, whatever lifestyle. Our ethical responsibility is all encompassing as is our sinfulness, but out of gratitude only rather than as a precursor for salvation. It follows that there is no condemnation for those who are united with Christ Jesus.

For Paul, the differences between us are a question of different gifts. God has dealt us different degrees of faith as well, all gifts. How does a Christian behave at the end of the day? For Paul, with hospitality, using one's gifts, loving even one's enemies (Rom. 12). What does this look like in daily life? A myriad of difference, for some eat everything, others don't. It's not our behaviors but our love for each other, justice, peace, joy. The question is not so much the *what* of our behaviors but the effect they have on others. Building up the common life of Christians is the goal (Rom. 14). As if in keeping with the situation and the call of Christ, Paul applies this by commending Phoebe and other women to the ministry of the new churches in Rome, whereas he seems to condemn women speaking in 1 Corinthians.

What about 1 Corinthians, the epistle that seems to have Paul ranting about all things moral?

First Corinthians

In reading Paul it is helpful to have Derrida close at hand. It is helpful to listen to the schism in Paul that reflects the schism always present in a Christian, the Paul who upbraids the small Corinthian church, telling them to root out the immoral (1 Cor. 5:13) and then in the same letter says "Love is patient; love is kind" (1 Cor. 13:4). It is helpful to read Paul *as* the church, divided even in itself. It is unhelpful to read Paul as though we really understand what he is saying, as though reading him were not the work of excavation, with many layers, historical, theological, linguistic, perhaps psychoanalytic. It is particularly unhelpful to read him as though he were using the same words as a "moral" preacher, for example, assuming that Paul meant by "immorality" or "prostitute" what *we think* in the twenty-first century he meant by "immorality" and "prostitute."

Halperin[2] writes about the differences in the very understanding of sex in Greek society. Sex was a way of instituting hierarchy. The roles understood were "passive" and "active" rather than homosexual and heterosexual. Whether female or male, the act of sex was a way of expressing one's superior social status and had little or nothing to do with intimacy. Paul was disgusted that men would use men in this way, when egalitarian community and love were to be the hallmarks of Christian life. "The husband does not have authority over his own body, but the wife does" (1 Cor. 7:4). Even in intensely patriarchal times, Paul warns of a necessity for commitment, the protection of marriage for women.

Clearly the community at Corinth was deeply troubled and surrounded by a pagan culture, and the preeminent fear was that the call of Christ would become for this struggling church simply the call of the world. This is the same temptation we face always as church. Paul's call was back to Christ's call, as Paul understood it, back from what was another religion, a religion where prostitutes were priests and sexuality was used as a sort of opiate. The call was to return to faithfulness to the triune God of the early Christian communities.

And so perhaps is our call. Our call is away from the gods of secularity, the gods that would have us worship at the shrine of hedonism and forgo the work of Christian community, the gods that would have us "use" others as things instead of loving others as neighbors. The issues here are not about homosexuality as we understand that word or our versions of sexual correctness, whatever they may look like, but about faithfulness and love for one another. Paul speaks of building Christian community in a world that aims to tear it apart.

But lest we explain away Paul, may we see him also as we see the text itself: contradictory, sometimes chaotic, self-aggrandizing (1 Cor. 4:15), self-effacing (1 Cor. 2:1), judgmental (1 Cor. 6:2), nonjudgmental (1 Cor. 4:1–5), loving (1 Cor. 4:14), and casting Christians to Satan (1 Cor. 5:5)? We see Paul and love him as fully and completely human, therefore sinful, but because of his master, able to accomplish miracles. Always the thread is to heal the divisions in the church at Corinth, heal the wounds and protect it from the defeat of the world.

---

2. David Halperin, *One Hundred Years of Homosexuality* (New York: Routledge, 1990), 30.

Yet also, the threads of protectionism are already evident. In the clos-ing of the church's doors against the gods of the world, perhaps Paul also closed them against the potential return of Christ. Paul is most assuredly the one who would ask of the Messiah at the gate, "When will you come?"[3]

As we read Paul's epistles, we read our own struggles; the letters that are sent are also sent to us. We should and shall and do respond down through the centuries. We, as with all scripture, write back. We remember that this is also proximate witness to the One and is not the One.

I found myself with others at the helm of the queer ship of our church, finding our greatest conversation partner in (the writings of) Paul. Paul was a true brother, suffering the same inner and outer divi-sions that we also experienced in church life. Like us, he was perhaps too easily disgusted at the habits of other people, eloquent and moral-istic, loving and angry, hurt and hurtful. Rather than eliminate him from our own canon, his writings were central to it. Paul was our first practice of welcoming those whom we might find strange. We loved to wrestle with welcoming the very foundation builder, as he prided himself on being, of our faith (1 Cor. 2:10). We loved to see Paul as queer (complicated, estranged, rejected, marginalized, contradictory).

Marriage Beginnings

In Pauline fashion, we found ourselves living out of a different, queer ethic. We tried to answer the call of the evangelos/stranger/queer who arrived. We attempted, as he did, to be faithful to the radical Christ, the antimorality Christ we read about in scripture. We tried to be countercultural in his manner.

We performed North America's first legally recognized same-sex marriage[4] as disciples of Christ behaving queerly. That is, when the couple came to see me and asked to be married, I assumed them to be adults like any other adults. I assumed that they had been called into love with each other like any other adults who came to me asking for marriage. They appeared to love each other as did other couples.

3. See p. 180 and the discussion of Blanchot's parable.
4. See note 2 on p. 18.

The only reference Jesus made to marriage was to decry divorce, in other words to *reform* the marriage laws of his day in favor of the rights of women (Mark 10:2–12). We recognized that Paul, contrary to his times, recommended that a man is better off having no relations with a woman. However, the overriding principle for Paul was not any particular state of marriage but following God. As he says in 1 Corinthians: "Let each of you lead the life that the Lord has assigned, to which God called you. This is my rule in all the churches" (7:17).

The two women before me were together when the Lord called them into the church and into the state of matrimony. In a very real way, I saw no reason to separate what God had brought together. Neither did I see this as a matter for our church council or elders or worship leaders. I had never consulted or been asked to consult with them for any other marriage. They would all be privy to the announcement when I made it publicly with a reading of the Banns, a tradition Metropolitan Community Church Toronto had made famous with same-sex couples.

The reading of the Banns, however, did not make the marriage legal. The Banns form needed to be registered at the registry office by a clerk. I checked the form over carefully and so did our secretary. At no time did the form state male or female, nor define bride and groom as male and female. We read the announcement without a hitch and performed the marriage just as MCCT had done. I then sent the form off to the registry department where a clerk registered the marriage for the first time in North America. Some would have deemed this a mistake on the part of the clerk. We considered it an act of grace.

Of course, when it became publicly apparent (a daily newspaper did a story on it, complete with a photograph of the license) the registry department threatened to take away my license to marry despite the fact that I had broken no law. The issue became a national news moment when it broke on radio. Thanks to the broadcasting corporation and a lawyer involved in the struggle for same-sex marriage equality, I received a letter of apology within a week. Most important, the marriage remained legal.

I was asked to preach on the matter and decided to focus on the antiheterosexuality that I saw throughout scripture. It was through a heterosexual couple that sin came into the world after all, and Paul clearly thought it a less graced association than celibacy. I also attempted to exegete the passages that had been the bane of queer existence as I have in this study. The sermon wasn't universally acclaimed. Congregants made their way to my office with complaints and accolades, and I as well as others delighted in the level of scriptural debate that ensued. After all, we were living with difference. Ours was not an LBGT congregation. We represented a gamut of lifestyles and queerness.

The joy was that those who took part in the discussion, who examined their own lives in light of this action on behalf of three of their members in the name of Christ, changed and grew even though we still did not all agree. When our church voted on becoming officially Affirming a year later, there was not one dissenting vote on council.[5] Meanwhile queer folk feeling more invited by the action than ever continued to arrive. One said, "It's not enough to say your church is open or affirming. Before we were willing to walk in the door we wanted to see the church risk at least as much as we did by coming here."

That our church did risk was evident by the nature of the complaints I heard and the hate mail I began to receive. We risked losing members. We risked being targeted. We did lose members, and we were targeted. (It was not uncommon to have a protester attend service and hand out literature or posters immediately outside.) Those who stayed did so cognizant as perhaps never before of what it meant to be a member of our church.

Surprisingly, stereotypes were broken regarding who stayed and who didn't. Again, the queer continuum showed itself to be the best predictor and nothing else. An Albanian Muslim family came and asked to attend our introduction to Christianity classes. They converted and stayed. They said that they had had enough of prejudice and hatred. They spoke of the welcome and the openness to difference. We heard from them and from many others the same sentiment. "If you can accept and marry two queers, trans folk, then you can accept me, queer as I have felt."

---

5. The United Church had amended the process to make it a vote by council. Affirming meant that not only were we open to welcoming an LBGT, but we were also open to having an LBGT person in paid and accountable ministry. Shortly after we hired a spiritual director who was a lesbian.

I, who would never proselytize to another faith, who tried my best to connect them with their own tradition, baptized them, however reluctantly. Just like Philip, just like Ananias.

A Jewish businessman, conservative politically, began to attend. This puzzled our increasingly queer-conscious congregation until he brought his business partner who had just come out as transgender. Again, despite my misgivings and concerns that he connect with his own faith, I found myself welcoming him and baptizing him, and welcoming her.

Something was happening that had very little to do with me, and it seemed to us, a great deal to do with the movement of the Holy Spirit in our midst.

Chapter Eleven

Qu(e)erying Church

Beginning with the Church

What then is a church? What should a church be? What were we becoming at Emmanuel Howard Park? Were we a "true" church? Insists Karl Barth:

> It is important to note that the Church is not formed by a human gathering of people who would have the same opinions, but by a divine convocation that constitutes into a corps of individuals until then scattered at the mercy of their opinions.[1]

Ecclesia means assembled convocation. Calvin calls it a "company," emphasizing that as in the military it is made up of those called to service. The church is constituted in holiness, which is a setting apart from the world of other communities.

Barth again,

> The term "holy" applied to the Church, to God's work, and to believers has then no direct moral meaning. It does not mean that these people are particularly suited to come near to God, to deserve his revelation, that these things are particularly adapted to represent God. Rather, holiness is conferred upon them as a matter of the fact that God has chosen them, both men and things, in order to reveal himself in them.[2]

He continues,

> The Church, being different from any other human community, thereby is catholic, that is universal. She is linked by no barrier, either of state, or of race, or of culture. Exclusively and properly belonging to no one, the Church belongs to everyone.[3]

---

1. Karl Barth, *The Faith of the Church* (New York: Meridian Books, 1958), 136.
2. Ibid., 138.
3. Ibid., 139.

And: "The Church announces the Kingdom of God, she is not the Kingdom of God."[4]

Yet Barth seems in some of his writing, by calling the church the body of Christ, perilously close to considering her the kingdom. For what is the kingdom of God if not also that which is made manifest in the body and person of Jesus Christ?

Equating the church with God is a favorite pastime of theologians. John Milbank writes: " . . . and if Christians ask 'What is God like?' then they can only point to our 'response' to God in the formation of community. The community is what God is like."[5]

Although Milbank problematizes this by describing church as both God and also not God since made up of humans, we are frighteningly close to a merging of the two. Surely church is *never* Jesus Christ and *never* the kingdom. We are a communion of saints no doubt, as Barth goes on to describe them, both those who through the Word have been set apart for the acts of preaching, sacraments, commissioning, all *service*.[6] No saint is the same as Jesus Christ.

Yet Jesus Christ is both human and divine according to biblical witness. Then could not the church reflect Christ as both human and divine? Certainly insofar as she is both humble and also glorious in announcing the kingdom. *But she is not that which she announces.* She is a community that lives in hope. But she is not that hope. She is *not* Jesus Christ. Barth warns of glorifying or despising the church.[7]

It seems to me very biblical that Del and Mary did not just ask to be included anywhere but asked to be included in the church, and equally biblically that the movement toward the church as toward scripture is a movement toward Christ. But so might the movement of the church out to Del and Mary be the movement toward Christ, since Christ is not necessarily resident in either venue.

Paul speaks of the life of the faithful, the life of the church: "It is no longer I who live, but it is Christ who lives in me; and the life I now live in the flesh I live by faith in the Son of God, who loved me and

---

4. Ibid.
5. John Milbank, "Postmodern Critical Augustinianism: A Short Summa in Forty-two Responses to Unasked Questions," in *The Postmodern God: A Theological Reader,* ed. Graham Ward (Oxford: Blackwell, 1997), 269.
6. Barth, *Faith of the Church,* 138.
7. Ibid., 149.

gave himself for me" (Gal. 2:20). The statement is both belief and all that needs be said about life in the communion of the saints. This is a forgiven life. It is a life of the branch at one with the vine. But it still isn't Paul saying that he is Jesus Christ.

One of the first liturgical acts of worship as we gather is the prayer of confession followed by the assurance of forgiveness. The church then begs forgiveness as part of its raison d'être, just as it points to forgiveness in a way that the world never can. The humility of the church is critical. Christ sits at the head of the church as a ruler sits on a throne. The ruler's council is not the ruler. The church is not Christ. Too often we see ourselves as the body under the direction of the head or the hands and feet of Christ. May we constantly remind ourselves, out of love for ourselves and our neighbors, that we are not the hands, feet, or face of Christ. Thank God, we are not God.

Neither should we be self-loathing. We are to love our neighbor *as ourselves*, hence we are humble but not self-abasing. We do point to glory. We are among the proximate witnesses to the good news. There is something church has to give Del and Mary. There is also something Del and Mary have to give the church, even as they are church.

What then should church be like? What should the experience of church be like? The early church as depicted in Acts is a fractious place. Paul's epistles seem to be in part attempts to patch up rifts, correct, teach, and encourage. Within two decades of Christ's death there are churches, or communities of Christians, in Corinth, Antioch, Ephesus, and finally Rome.

Early rifts between Hellenic and Jewish Christians (Acts 6:1) and the issue of whether Christians needed to be circumcised seemed to lead to the Council of Jerusalem, where Peter and Paul represented two different opinions. At this council, Paul's argument won and the church decided around inclusion, and notably inclusion of those who were not similar genitally, inclusion of those who were considered by some to be unclean in their very person.

The early church was far from uniform on many topics, however, and we have little or no evidence of their worship or life except that they tended to share their wealth, share in the sacraments (however those were performed), and share in the persecution that was meted out to them almost immediately.[8]

Their diversity is interesting, and despite their differences and perhaps because of their shared persecution, they still exhibited a great deal of *koinonia* (communion).

Their obedience, even to death, was remarkably uniform. Early Christians came into conflict with Rome over Roman practices of emperor worship. "Jesus is Lord" was (and is) a slogan they died for.

Even before Constantine's conversion in or around 313 AD, the second century saw approximately a half million Christians. The new faith had spread through Italy into Sicily and Sardinia, and to North Africa and then on to Spain, France, and the British Isles. Far from causing a drop in numbers, persecution simply forced Christians to become more itinerant. By the third century half a million had become five million, which quickly doubled to around ten million after Constantine's conversion.

It is not difficult to see why martyrdom and the sort of faith that would lead to martyrdom would also lead to expansion. The bravery of those who would not renounce Christ and went willingly to be burnt at stakes, fed to animals, or crucified could not fail to impress even their captors.

But if Acts is accurate in portraying the early Christian church as a place where widows were cared for, where the wealthy opened their homes to the poor, and where those who normally would consider each other unclean shared table fellowship, it is possible to see that not only martyrdom was appealing.

Feeding the poor both spiritually and physically, again extensive and inclusive hospitality, has been an aspect of the church since Christ himself modeled the behavior. Christ demanded in the lives of his followers astoundingly high commitment and an alternative lifestyle that must have seemed to their civilized Greek and Roman neighbors completely uncivilized. The distaste and aversion that Del and Mary are met with both institutionally and personally by Christians was the way Christians were met by first the Jews and then the Greeks and Romans.

---

8. Raymond E. Brown, *The Churches the Apostles Left Behind* (New York: Paulist Press, 1984).

The philosophical response to Christians hasn't changed much either. As an atheist, I had seen the Christian church as a moralist club run by rather simple people who accepted creedal statements that were ludicrous. My atheist friends and I were typically Greek in that regard. The agenda for the characterization of Christians as simple-minded dates from the early church.

Christians have always been "fools" for Christ in the eyes of the world. Christians who are different, Christians who are queer, have a history of being welcomed into the early church, as the Ethiopian eunuch in Acts shows.

Those who are unclean, like women in the gospels; intersexed, like the eunuch; slaves, like Philemon, are all welcomed in this new communion. Importantly, in the early church, they were not just welcome to sit in the seats of a large building but were welcomed into the very homes of other Christians. They were welcomed around the dinner table as well as the table of Communion. There appears to have been mission work in the sense of money sent abroad or away, but the early disciples shared everything in common at home as well. Their own lives were often forfeited in a social way before martyrdom was called for.

The church in Acts and the Epistles is, we must admit, a radically different sort of social organization than our own institutions. Even before persecution became the early churches' dominant theme, the first-century churches practiced a highly committed, radically inclusive form of community. This was not a community in withdrawal from the dominant culture, however, but one that went out teaching, preaching, and healing.

Beginning Again with the Church

As we listened to Del's words and Mary's words, as readers, we might try to imagine them sitting on our boards in our church contexts or deciding liturgical issues or spending mission dollars in our home congregations. We might try to imagine what a committee would look like and function like that could include them.

We at Emmanuel Howard Park learned from our experience of doing just that. We welcomed them on our committees and boards. We trusted them in spending money. We did invite them into our own homes, and to share dinner with our children.

One of the first lessons we learned was what passes as acceptable small talk. Del's and Mary's openness about their lives inspired others to be open about their faults as well. Del would often speak of needing a "joint" (a marijuana cigarette) after vacation Bible school. Our younger parents whose children were in vacation Bible school, and had probably had some experience with marijuana themselves, laughed uneasily at first and later shared some of their own drug experiences.

Mary, serving Communion, had even some evening service people disturbed. Many, having seen Communion as a solemn affair in the past, wanted to laugh at her outrageous dress, heels, and hair and ended up smiling a lot. This led to a much more joyous Eucharist when Mary served, a joy that we discussed around coffee later, as more theologically and biblically appropriate.

Discussions over finances were decidedly different when Del or Mary were in attendance. Spending large amounts on the church's interior suddenly seemed less necessary and spending more money on outreach and food seemed more urgent. Once our larger donors got to know the individuals from the evening service, some expenses that might seem strange to other finance committees seemed less strange.

For example, we agreed to pay Del $150 for a pay-as-you-go cell phone. It was impossible for her to get any musical jobs without a phone, and since Del had no credit rating, no phone company would install one without a huge down payment. We agreed to do this because we knew Del. At other times we paid for phone bills, rent, clothes for congregants. We had three to five people working in various part-time capacities around the church so that they could qualify for an extra transportation allowance on their welfare check, and those working were considered staff.

It's a great deal easier to agree to pay for any or all of the above when those who are requesting it are sitting across from you at the table when the decision is made. Other payments become more difficult. For instance, street people would often come to the church asking for cash with this or that reason, people whom we did not know and were not part of our evening or morning service. The Outreach Committee decided that most of the money given under such circumstances went to the purchase of crack cocaine. They knew this for a fact, because they knew the people involved. We stopped dispensing charity that way and made it a policy that benevolent gifts were to go through the Outreach Committee.

As evening service people sat on the Worship Committee, more experimental worship styles were tried, ones that included their talents and ideas. For example, Del and I performed a "John X John" service with the music of John Coltrane and the gospel of John. We found overhead projections and repetitious refrains more conducive to singing for a congregation that was often illiterate or unable to afford prescription glasses. Later we moved to a Taizé-style worship with simple musical refrains repeated. "Amazing Grace," the perennial favorite, was sung as one verse (the first) repeated over and over. Services were less formal and more interactive, and that spirit also began to seep into the morning service.

Del became an extended member of my own family, dropping over after services from time to time, discussing new musical releases with my son, inviting us out to hear jazz or blues. Two other members of the evening service regularly attended a Family Games Night, and many showed up to have their pictures taken for our church directory. This was a great source of frustration for the photography company which hoped to sell photo packages. As one after another of the perilously poor lined up for the camera, it became clear not many would be purchasing anything.

When we opened the doors of our church and our families, more traditionally middle-class church members learned that this meant changing many of the ways we had traditionally conducted the business of church. We were forced by our faithfulness to live inclusively.

Mark's Church[9]

The history of church, of course, is also scriptural. There are antecedents to our own limited experience. The early church realities in some ways mirrored our own.

---

9. Keith A. Russell, *In Search of the Church* (New York: Alban Institute, 1994). Much of my historical information in this section and the following comes from Russell's research.

Mark's gospel was most likely written during the Roman occupation of Palestine. The Jewish elite was composed of the Sadducees who hoped to appease Rome by cooperation, the Pharisees who desired reform within Judaism itself and opposed cooperation, the Essenes who practiced and preached a more radical separation from both Rome and official Judaism, and finally the Zealots who proposed armed insurrection.

Mark countered with another sort of alternative entirely. Jewish Christians approached all other groups with the cross of Christ as a symbol of nonaligned resistance: engaged unlike the Essenes, yet equally critical of Jewish leadership; anti-Rome, yet undermining Roman authority not with revolution but with an alliance with Christ.

Alternative communities needed to sow the seeds of faith and wait patiently (4:1–34). With the power of the cross the enemies were overcome, even though historically very little had changed. The cross was not the symbol of a victim of Rome but of one triumphant over all earthly powers. Christians were called to healing in the now, not in some future time, but while still under domination. In this healing also came the power to resist all earthly principalities. Its assurance was apocalyptic. The end was liberation.

This alternative community needed discipline. Worship was a daily event, as was education, because otherwise the determination to live out of resistance would be lacking. Urgency was central to all that happened. A constant education to strengthen against the cultural trends was critical for survival.

Matthew's Church

Mark's was not the only church experience. As Jewish Christians established new worshiping communities, variations on that theme developed.

As Mark seemed to have been written with the marginalized in mind, Matthew's readers appeared to be wealthier. Some scholars[10] believe the book was written in the city of Antioch around 80–90 CE,

---

10. E.g., Keith A. Russell.

later than Mark's gospel. The language might have been shifting from Aramaic to Greek, and the society from rural to urban. Far more multicultural than Mark's church, Matthew's church needs to consider justice for the poor. Households must be rooted in Christ Jesus rather than in ethnicity, race, or class.

The beatitudes focus on teaching what this household might look like. The household is to be reviled, persecuted, peaceful, poor, mournful, and meek but hungry for justice and mercy. The household church was most likely then, as now, quite different than this ideal, but the aim of the community was to strive for hospitality. Disciples were to be received as if they were Christ himself. Mutuality was to be practiced as much as possible.

The test of justice in the household church was always its attitude of welcoming for the marginalized. Individual conversion was always communal in its implication, and the implications of this were a high-demand Christianity. One's life was at stake, and one was definitely outside of any "comfort" zone.

Luke's Church

Luke's audience was mainly Greek, converted from some sort of Roman religious view. They were reliant on secondary sources for witness to the death and resurrection of Christ. They were most likely under siege and unrecognized as an official religion. It has long been a consensus among scholars that Luke and Acts had the same author and therefore the same view and experience of church.

Jesus' temptations in Luke (4:3–12) involve a "political" temptation. Jesus could have chosen a political or military solution (4:5–6). This surely was what many of the Jews of Jesus' day longed for. But the "magical/miracle" options were all denied. The route to the kingdom was going to be longer and slower than that.

The poor and marginalized in Luke are not the object of justice or a necessary component of the church but were, in fact, the *honored* of the church (23:55–24:12). The first witnesses of the resurrection were women, arguably the most oppressed of the era. The church was profoundly countercultural in that roles in it were a reversal of those found under Roman rule. The church modeled itself after what heaven might look like.

As "signs of things promised," Luke's church was to be as if it were the kingdom, perhaps always failing, but always attempting. Luke's church did not point to "pie in the sky when you die" but tried to live "pie now!" The wealthy tithed to the poor. Keith Russell states, "In truth, many [middle-class] Christians [today] are tithing but it is to Visa or MasterCard."[11] Luke was attentive to the issues of stewardship. It was important to reverse the cultural imperatives to be able to create a community that would not only sustain life for some but nurture it enough to resist whatever persecution threatened. Faith could then be founded on the experience as well as the stories of Christ's compassion.

I recall saying to a colleague that it's easy to fill a church if that is all we want to do. Just feed people. Imagine, the evening service and people like Del and Mary taught me, what it would be like to really love, help, feed, and house the poor, not just pay somebody else to? We had effectively doubled the number of those attending services in our sanctuary in one year by feeding them, first food, then everything else that we could offer. Until, that is, "they" became "us."

Paul's Church

Even Paul's church was a church of the hunted, the outlawed, the suspect sustained by those with enough wealth to do so. This latest scriptural look at what church must have been show that Paul's images of church are primarily that of reconciling community (Rom. 5:6–11; 2 Cor. 5:16–21; Eph. 2:11–21) and body of Christ (Rom. 12:1–21; 1 Cor. 12:1–31; Eph. 4:1–16).[12]

In the reconciling vision, one was to convert personally and then almost immediately to develop a new social identity. This new community and identity was over and against the world of power but also as part of the body of Christ, a new world to be confirmed. The new world's reality was always fraught with danger and difficulty and was, being human, always flawed.

---

11. Russell, *In Search of the Church*, 49.
12. Ibid., 53.

The struggle and challenge evoked by the very need for the epistles was the Christian journey. Outreach focused on enacting church. We did not go out to "do" to them but invited "them" in to "do" with us. Inward looking meant looking at all the problems of the marginalized because "we" were marginalized. Even if these early communities had wealthy members, they were sharing the wealth to such a degree that distinctions of class became blurred. Persecution also made social division less important.

For Paul's church, charity was home. He was sustained, as were all members, by other members.

Peter's Church

The converts in 1 Peter were both Jews and non-Jews, although Gentiles outnumbered Jews. First Peter was composed in Asia Minor for circulation around Christian household churches in four provinces of the Roman Empire. Most addressed were displaced workers living in the diaspora, and so church became home for the displaced.

The displaced were the new "priesthood" (2:9–10). It is critical to make sense of the suffering of those who have forsaken their old lives and households and chosen this new household of God or church. First Peter reminds believers that it is in their suffering that they are most like Christ. The already suffering, the already marginalized, were already living the Christian life. Now they were given hope, and they were given status. Church was a home for the homeless.

Churches in the twenty-first century are used to doing mission *to* the homeless. That is, programs exist that allow homeless to sleep in churches, eat in churches, and get money from churches for a variety of programs and direct needs. Many churches see the marginalized as their reason for existence. Anyone is allowed to come to service. But how many churches in the first world *consist* of the homeless, the dispossessed? How many churches see it as their reason for existence to become a church consisting of the dispossessed?

John's Church

Far from the comfortable pews of many North American congregations, biblical communities gathered around Christ were coming together for protection from the world around them. Like 1 Peter, the Apocalypse of John was most likely written in Asia Minor for the approximately eighty thousand Christians living there.[13] John wrote it under house arrest.

The dispossessed lower classes, of which Christians were mainly composed, were also suspected of being potential revolutionaries. John's Christian communities were communities in crisis. Resistance to overt oppression was necessary for survival. They felt themselves to be in a spiritual "Babylon," a place of humility and danger. Jerusalem and apocalypse were the promise for enduring unimaginable terror. Any idea of accommodation to the regime which hunted and persecuted them daily was anathema.

Today we live in an era when Christians are still seen as representing and being represented by the power elites in North America. Rather than a church over and against power in all its secular manifestations, the church is often seen as just another face of that self-same power. Much talk is given to the poor, especially the inner-city poor, but it is often preached to congregations that are demographically anything but.[14]

A glance over those who make up the audiences of most evangelicals on television in North America, for example, will feature, whether people of color or not, individuals with suits and ties, dresses and professionally cut hair. I search, as have many in our Outreach Committee, for transgenders, for street people, for "crazies," as Mary calls them.[15] That most of those attending are working class may be true, but that they are the poorest of the poor appears not to be true.

Not only do most congregations eschew the crazies and queers, but increasingly they alienate everyone. Despite the power wielded by the voice of the Christian right, the pews of Christian churches are emptying out. Douglas John Hall, in his book *The Future of the*

---

13. Ibid., 79.
14. Reginald Bibby, *Unknown Gods: The Ongoing Story of Religion in Canada* (Toronto: Stoddart, 1993).
15. Conversation with the author, September 10, 2000.

Church, lists four reactions to what he calls the "humiliation of the church" on the part of church leaders. The first is to deny that the mainline churches in North America are shrinking. Indeed, between 1900 and 2000 Protestantism in the United States shrank from two-thirds of the population to one-third despite the individual success of some parishes.[16]

Second, they attempt to recover Christendom. This would include the "marketers" who stress "how tos" and revivals. They would agree that Christendom has been decimated but avow that liberalism, humanism, ordaining homosexuals, etc., etc., are the culprits. Or one might add to Hall, that televangelists, fundamentalists, literalists have ruined everything.

Third, Hall says leaders behave "as if" all is well, and we can lose members at the current rate and all will still be well. We turn inward and try to survive this generation, or our years to retirement or until a better job comes along. We pretend that the church is fine.

Fourth, and Hall states the only biblically legitimate option, is to try and find understanding in the current belittlement — in a sense, to faithfully see God's hand at work even in this embattled state. Hall recommends substituting a theology of the cross for a theology of glory. He even speculates that the church's humiliation may be positive or providential. Hall sees this era as a special invitation to discipleship.

Counter to Hall, or at least acting perhaps as a corrective, is Reginald Bibby's assertion that:

> If there are some observers who want to argue that things go in cycles and that all will eventually be well, there are others who insist on downplaying the numbers. At their worst, some people in this camp simplistically dismiss people who are concerned about numbers as bean counters, and presumably embrace the idea that quality is more important than quantity. I would remind them that the quality-versus-quantity cliché may not have as much truth to it as one of its amendments: The mark of quality is not necessarily the absence of quantity.[17]

---

16. Douglas John Hall, *The Future of the Church* (Toronto: United Church Publishing, 1989), 25.

17. Bibby, *Unknown Gods,* 102.

Bibby brings in William Willimon, former Duke University theologian, who says small numbers are no more symptomatic of faithfulness than large numbers. Willimon also states:

> We seem to lack something interesting to say that can't be heard elsewhere. That's deadly. It's usually interesting advice but the worst thing is that it's not any different advice than they could get at Rotary.[18]

Just because we're small doesn't mean we're truly Christian!

Perhaps, as in all issues related to Christ, here too the queer theologian has something to contribute. Perhaps, as Hall states, size doesn't matter, but obedience to Christ does. But, as Bibby and Willimon point out, neither does lack of size necessarily have anything to do with obedience.

Perhaps it is possible to grow and be faithful, or not, to shrink and be faithful, or not. What church is, then, is more important than the size of church! Bibby seems to speak of meeting the spiritual needs of churchgoers as if these should be important. As if spiritual needs were akin to hunger for food and the correct mix of buffet items would lure the famished. That people are famished spiritually is no doubt true, but perhaps the "food" of the gospel is as unpalatable now as it was then in first-century Christianity.

Perhaps Hall's call, if it is a call to high-commitment Christianity, is more biblically accurate — except that Hall's unwritten assumption seems to be that middle-class North Americans find Christianity just too high a commitment and therefore unpalatable for them. Perhaps, but what about the ones we are biblically mandated to welcome — the poor and dispossessed?

The queer church assumption is that the future of the church is irrelevant, and that has certainly been our experience in the evening service. God through Christ will triumph. This is faith's answer to anxiety about the state of the church. But it is not an excuse for unfaithfulness. The faithful will be called to feed and house and welcome around the table, to give over the church as we know it to its true owners, the most marginalized of all. If we can honestly say we are doing that, our queer experience is that the church will inevitably grow, because if the gift is real, it is rarely if ever refused.

---

18. Ibid., 245.

This then might please Bibby and the "marketers" but only if their concern is people and not dollars. The church of the poor will most likely be a poor church. Or maybe not. One of our discoveries liturgically is that the evening service wanted and needed to give an offering and was, comparatively speaking, more generous than the morning service. Another experience was that the preaching needed to affirm over and over again that those assembled "owned" the church that they were in, that ordered clergy worked for them, and that the assembled people had not just a voice, but *the* voice. This, like a theological drumbeat, had to be affirmed again and again, as the ecclesiological version of "Christ died for you/me!"

At first the sermon was, for most if not all, empty words. We had to make it real in polity, community, and worship. We had to trust "them" with the money as well as make speeches about it. We had to feed them. We had to welcome them into our celebrations and homes. We had to trust property and sacrament, body and soul to them until "they" became "us." From the first, those of us who were more typical churchgoers knew this was risky and that it would cost. It was and it did. The risk was in seeing ourselves as "them." The cost was to become a high-commitment Christianity.

Meal preparation is as time consuming as sermon preparation and every week found us scrounging for food and facing the challenge of feeding from forty to one hundred people. Often paranoid schizophrenics and epileptics had to be cared for at these meal times. Such high pastoral needs of evening service members necessitated adding additional staff, usually from our evening service. Outreach meetings where evening service members dominated had to be less structured and held around times convenient to those who had often lost their sense of chronological time. Property fears of older members and personal safety issues regarding children were real and needed to be discussed. Staff meetings where our part-time welfare-receiving staff were welcome had to be more solicitous and encouraging so that the seldom heard could be heard.

To walk in the shoes of the marginalized if only for a few blocks was often difficult. I attended Mary's graduation ceremony from her first experience of rehabilitation. Even in the drug addicted and formerly addicted that were the majority of the audience, I noticed sniggering and dismissal. When she, another transgender, and I went for coffee afterwards, none of the staff sat with us. None of the other graduates asked for her phone number.

Another time, walking with her along a major street, where she was met with cat calls, leers, and abuse, I asked her what it was like to put up with that every time she set foot outside. "You get used to it, honey!" she answered. I never did.

To the psychiatrized, the hated, the crazy, the queer, every step "outside" can be painful. Church can and should be a haven, instead of another hurdle. Morning service people had to learn to act unshocked. They had to learn not to question twice when two women described one woman as the other mother and stated that there was no "father."

Conversely, evening service people had to learn to trust "straights" again and to be patient with their discomfort. The "gift" of Christian community had to be compelling enough for each group to learn to tolerate the other. This demanded a great deal of one-on-one pastoral care and the care of the Congregation Committee (elders). The committee learned to stretch its understanding and to work more faithfully than any other Congregation Committee I had ever witnessed.

Staff had to understand "call" as going far beyond the "professionalism" that clergy had become used to. They had to do this while becoming more aware of their own limits, issues, and codependent habits. "They" becoming "us" did not mean there was no difference or that we had to become the same or that "they" were better than we. It meant scrupulous but compassionate honesty about our own issues and addictions.

To answer Bibby's challenge to the church, we attempted to be all things to the people who needed us most. We attempted to do this by raising Christ again as the focus of the church. We attempted to reenact early household churches by becoming more high commitment than any other church we had ever experienced. Over and over stewardship was emphasized, as was our commitment to a community whose only reason was loving God and neighbor.

To answer Hall's challenge: we were radically inclusive, therefore faithful, and went out of our way to include and attract those too frightened to set foot inside a church. We attempted to be radically countercultural. I invited Mary and Del and many other marginalized to be on a radio show I hosted once a month on university radio. We took part in demonstrations and sat on boards for food banks, low-cost banking, and prisoners' rights. We did it not as liberals or conservatives, but as Christians serving a queer Christ in a queer church.

The church it seemed, like Christianity itself, was neither/nor nor either/or. The aim was always to be invitational to all theological opinions, sociological circumstances, and economic backgrounds; in short, to all of *difference*. Everyone was welcomed, not just to anywhere, but to the table of Christ. Consequently we tried never to exclude, not even the political conservatives who in government, it would be easy to argue, had helped create poverty in our jurisdiction. We attempted never to preach a sermon that would belittle even the most homophobic literalist who might venture in. Violence in word or deed was not tolerated in our community, but difference was upheld as essential. This too was risky and costly. We failed frequently. We lost members. We succeeded often. We gained members.

What we attempted was to be nonjudgmental and, of course, we failed.

One major hurdle in this approach was the self-censorship of potential adherents. Many did not acclimatize well to such diversity and did not stay long enough to feel its benefits. We prayed for them and for ourselves. The other was our own anxiety about attaining anything, or being better at anything. Trusting that this is God's world was the ongoing unmet challenge.

We prayed most for the church — that is, both the body and not the body of Christ, both heaven and not heaven, inclusive and not inclusive, human and divine: Every evening service ended with " . . . in my church, Lord, be glorified." We sang this and extended our arms to encompass the entire assembly and, by way of the assembled, God's world. It intimated that we were not glorifying God as we should and that we should be glorifying God as we had not.

As such, we felt free to use research by "marketers" to reach the most marginalized. We felt free to dismiss the very marketers whose research we used as often theologically vacuous. We felt free to ignore advice or take it around issues of growth and relevance in the community. We felt free to interpret our own concern for numbers as lack of faith or faith depending on the situation and our own spirits. We felt free to experiment liturgically based on what vehicle seemed to be most faithful to God and neighbor even if it meant breaking all the rules of liturgy. Our Worship Committee's prime mandate was to develop worship that glorified God and inspired our people. That meant two very different services, evening and morning. And yet over time, the two infected each other to some degree. The morning service became more energized as more children came, and the evening service became less interactive as more people came. We were, for example, very quickly unable to have Communion around the table but had to revert to lines of people in the aisles due to the architecture of our space.

We reminded ourselves constantly that good news meant food and material help to our members as well as worship together as a community. It also meant a community that operated seven days a week. My home phone number appeared on my card, as did the numbers of our accountable staff. Retreats on Saturday were offered. Educational, personal, and political support was offered. We struggled with gifts or lack of them in our community. We would constantly remind ourselves that "so-and-so's gifts do not include reliability at this time." We said it with a smile, but we meant it.

Those who worked for us to supplement their social assistance were never upbraided for their unreliability but were simply noted as not appearing for the requisite fifteen hours that month. Each month was a new possibility. There was always work to do. If handouts were asked for by nonmembers, we would invite them to become members; "This is your church and if you come to the meeting of our Outreach Committee, you can spend your own money there in cooperation with the other owners of this church."

Behind this approach we hoped was the assumption that Christ owned and worked through the process by the person of the Holy Spirit. Humility needed to be the overriding operative ethic. We were all crazy at times. Some of us were crazy all the time. We needed to be gentle with each other. I needed to learn to be gentle with myself.

Members often, through imagined or real slights, left, sometimes returning, sometimes not. I reminded myself, they reminded themselves, that this was not about us but about them. Every day of our high-demand, high-needs church was an occasion for spiritual growth. We learned and taught each other perseverance, faithfulness, and gentleness. We also learned how far we were from all three in every moment.

I took solace in theory. I found myself constantly returning to those who were willing to live in the question. Our church, at all points, seemed in uncharted territory. No answers sufficed.

Chapter Twelve

Qu(e)erying the Gift

Beginning Again
with the Beginning, Again

As I despaired of finding guides or aides in writing on evangelism, Derrida and others who spoke of the impossibility of knowing truth or transmitting truth seemed eminently practical. Far from esoteric theory, French (and other) poststructuralists described better than "how to" manuals on church growth our everyday reality at Emmanuel Howard Park United.

Blanchot tells a story of the messiah standing at the gates of the city living unrecognized among the poorest of the poor. He says the only question we would rightly have of him is, "When will you come?"[1] Caputo, in his retelling, also says of Derrida that his work is in part an attempt to keep *tout autre* as *tout autre* (every other as wholly other). Justice for Derrida is the trace of what is to come beyond anything we can foreclose or know.

Evangelism for Derrida, as for us, comes from the outside in. The gift, for Derrida, is that which is not repaid, therefore nothing human. Although Derrida claims atheism, Christians might also agree that a gift, a true gift, exacts no obligation, even gratitude. Therefore a gift, so to speak, must be outside time, must end time in a sense. It can only come, even as the voice of deconstruction says, from beyond the human, if at all. As Caputo goes on to say, "never to collapse the coming of the just one into the order of what is present or absent."[2]

---

1. John Caputo, *The Prayers and Tears of Jacques Derrida* (Bloomington: Indiana University Press, 1997), xxiv.
2. Ibid.

Whether we prefer Meister Eckhart ("I pray God to rid me of God"[3]) or Augustine ("What do I love when I love my God?"[4]), Christians can surely never claim knowledge of the Messiah other than that of a proximate witness of a proximate witness (our reading, scripture, story). That we acknowledge a messiah despite this is what we call faith. That we claim a gift given, a messianic presence as unknowable for its having already come as for its coming again, is also faith, a faith similar to the new faith like the presence of deconstruction itself. The difference is that Christians call this hope beyond hope "Christ," and claim it as a promise even though our doubt never ends.

As Christians in our queer church, we attempted to act as if everyone, but particularly those who were queer, might be Christ. That they were never quite Christ and that we never quite knew if they were Christ was the contextual setting for the movement of evangelism. That it is critical to *never know Christ* for us, as for Derrida, necessitates some explanation, for it is critical when we come to finally examine what a queer evangelist is, what queer theology might be. It is critical that Jesus Christ finally and always, in this life, be undecidable, unreachable — that as church, we can never speak *for* him but only *of* him and *to* him.

Derrida speaks of gratitude nullifying the giftedness of gifting. He says that even in anonymity, the knowing of the gifter nullifies the giftedness of gifting. In a sense, there is no way that we are freed from being recompensed for our "goodness." All we are doing, even at our best, is keeping some strange sort of economy of gifting going.

C. S. Lewis was reputed to have said something along the lines of "You can tell that she was a good woman. You could tell it from the hunted look in the recipients of her goodness' eyes."[5] That hunted look is the flip side of the glowing look of "having done the Lord's work" on the faces of benefactors everywhere (as well as inquisitors).

It is crucial that Christians understand that it is impossible to do "good" works. This may come as a shock to those who mean well, but it is the first of the shocks of the Christian life. Whether we stand

---

3. Ibid., 1.
4. Ibid., xxiv.
5. C. S. Lewis, quoted during a television broadcast with Rev. N. Gumbel, CBC, December 12, 1999.

in front of tanks in Tiananmen Square or work for no pay in third-world countries or answer calls on Saturday nights, we can do no good works!

The immediate protest is that our works may not be "good" in any transcendental sense, but surely our gifts, inadequate as they are, are better than doing nothing. Doing nothing is the great fear of Christians of the right or left. Of the left, we need to be actively "fighting the system." Of the right, we need to be purging our sinful lives. Derrida himself would argue that one must give economy its chance. But why?

Why should one take part in the struggle? Why should one get out of bed in the morning? Why? There is only one answer, which is the Christian's version of Levinas's command in the introduction: because we are called to do so by the Other. As such, we are only answering the call. It is not particularly admirable. Perhaps it is more admirable than turning over and going back into the land of Lethe, perhaps not. We are, to be sure, not the judge of this one. Another profoundly Christian conclusion. As Jesus said, "So you also when you have done all that you were ordered to do, say, 'We are worthless slaves; we have done only what we ought to have done!'" (Luke 17:10).

In the popular understanding of evangelism, we possess the good news of Christ and we give the news to you, and through the grace of God you accept or reject. If you accept, all rejoice. If you reject, heaven and earth weep. If we apply the logic of biblical lore or deconstruction (which are surprisingly similar), God calls and God accepts or not. Are we automatons? No, because we can follow what God does or not. The only "directional," if you will, choice that a Christian makes is to assent or not. The only exercise of *free* will is obedience to God's will.

The result should be an ease in our anxiety levels and an increase in our anxiety levels. Because if we are claimed yet free, or rather, free to be claimed, where is the gift still?

The gift is the very claiming. The gift is the opportunity for obedience to the absolutely undecidable. Perhaps there are no easy answers ever. This can be seen as freedom and as joy, this claim upon us. There is no greater debt, a completely unpayable debt and no greater freedom.

It is simply another restatement of the biblical idea of gift. It is a gift we never asked for and a far greater gift than we can ever repay. Yet a gift we do not need to accept, a gift that we can take or leave as if it were not a gift. The gift is, take it and be forever in debt or do not take it. The gift is a first-century Jew upon a cross who is, the gifter claims, God. Christ died for you but only if you agree that he died for you. You only agree to bow down if it is God's wish. You bow down freely before this Christ. You choose to not bow down. Freedom is manifest, however, only if you do. Bondage is to choose not to recognize the Divine. But only if you acknowledge this concept of freedom is it freedom, and only then have you lost any freedom. Choose to lose choice. That is your only choice, if you choose it. That is freedom.

Only do what is impossible. This is how the queer Christian bows down. This is the queerness in the movement of our faith. This is how queer theology might work or unwork itself. What does it look like to pray to Christ, through Christ to God? There is surely no pure prayer as there is no pure anything, even pure impurity. However there *is* prayer. Prayer is an answer to the call from the other and the Other (God). It is an answer back. Again, it is not ours. For as soon as we agree to pray, we agree that prayer is God's prayer to God's self. God answers all prayer because only God prays to God. We are, like branches to the vine, a circuit wire through which God answers God. Our choice again is to lose choice and claim that loss as freedom.

A professor once told me that freedom of choice to a Christian was like a bystander watching a young child about to be hit by a car. The bystander's choice consisted of swooping her clear of the oncoming vehicle or not. To think there is choice in such a circumstance is the loss of freedom.[6] Perhaps it is the place of evil, that sort of choice?

But even this is not as simple as it sounds at first. I, as bystander, may have six children at home for whom I am the sole support, and in risking my life for one child, I risk the six children. Or I may simply go into shock and, as in a dream, be unable to move quickly enough. I may not care at all about the child's life and be thinking of the title

---

6. Professor David Demson at a lecture circa 1994, Emmanuel College, University of Toronto.

of hero that will be mine by making a relatively safe move. I may be concerned about what the other bystanders would think of me if I did not move, far more than of the child at all. Is this then acting in concert with the will of God?

Like gift giving, human action is always ambivalent. We cannot speak for Christ or act as Christ would. This grounds us in a permanent state of humility (and reality). There are no holy ones, only ones that point to the holy. Or as Derrida might say, justice is deconstruction. The space must always be left for the "not yet." There will always be a question. Even this question might give way to certainty, as in the second coming of Christ.

Queer theology might want to say that Christ precedes essence and existence. That, to reverse Levinas's claim that every discourse must justify itself in front of philosophy that was quoted in the first chapter, we might want to say that every discourse must justify itself before God (or as Derrida might say — justice or the not-yet). Before God, every discourse will be found wanting, even the discourse of scripture. For scripture also speaks *about* and not for.

The church, we discovered in practice and theologically speaking, is an ambivalent place. It still, however, needs to exist "as if" Christ calls it into being; as if we, as Christian community, knew what God wanted of us; as if we were capable of enacting that call; as if we loved each other; as if we were Christian; as if we had something to offer. Could this be what obedience looks like?

To do even this requires that we do the opposite of what we would like to do most of the time. Naturally we don't like to be face to face with pain and poverty. We don't much like to work hard or be nice to people with whom we have nothing in common. To do this requires the actions of the Holy Spirit. We don't want to choose obedience. We don't want to choose freedom. We don't want to be chosen.

The Impossibility of the Gift as Lived

The "as if" approach of our congregation also invites a queer answer to the question of pluralism. Since we must never exclude or speak *as* Christ, we can certainly never speak against our neighbors on the basis of their religious beliefs. We must admit to them as to all that we have no answers. We do not and will never know what Christ would say to a Muslim or Wiccan or Hindu. Our only clues are that Christ would include, heal, love. Christ was a Jew, so of necessity we are "honorary Jews." Christ incarnate might speak to us through a Muslim or any other neighbor. We need to be on guard for the one at the gates, to be in listening mode.

Practically, this has meant, in our church, to pray and most often pray for healing. Our prayers, even when prayers of thanksgiving, were prayers of healing. The addiction paradigm was one that we often spoke of since many of our members had or were struggling with addiction. Our own addictiveness became a metaphor for our separation from God, an acknowledgment that, left to ourselves, we would always try to substitute something for God as Lord of our lives. We would always rather be obedient to a drug's call or family or status or money or to any seemingly solid "thing" than to the call of Christ.

Whatever the struggle looked like to free ourselves from the call of our particular drug was also what it looked like to free ourselves for the call of God. Any twelve-step follower will know that this is one of the most arduous spiritual journeys. Conversion as process meant for all of us a great deal of work, transformation, and challenge. Addiction, or lack, seemed to us structural in the human creature. This made it an even better metaphor for our distance from any accomplishable goal. Hour by hour, step by step, we assisted each other with the affirmation that there were no failures in our congregation. The "gift" of community, love and support was never contingent upon anything but being there.

Interviewing Del for a radio show on public radio, I kept making the mistake of using the masculine pronoun. Del looks very male so that despite the conversation being about transgender issues, my very speech spoke more than I could about the problems of the transgendered. More than once Del corrected me; more than once I referred to her as "he." In the very communication between us, I was subtly and not so subtly being evangelized. Del was teaching me how to see and speak queerly.

Teaching us as church how to be with the marginalized, teaching us how we were marginalized, teaching the marginalized how to be with the church and also teaching the church how to become marginalized, all these were part of the economy of gift giving which is the economy of evangelism. The movement starts from the outside, moves through and to us, moves from us, but never completes itself, never finds home. It always accrues meaning, remains fluid. Evangelism, like the economy of the gift, never is successful, never fails. No one is ever evangelized or evangelizes, except to give the economy of evangelism its chance. The movement starts with God and ends God alone knows where.

In small and large ways we who are all different learned how to "be" with difference, how to let it alone but not to retreat into isolation, how to question difference. We began the practice of asking difference about itself. I began over the course of this study to realize that we, as church, have been as crippled by our politeness, our guilt, as by our queer-phobia. Jesus told us to become like children, and the process was to become childlike in our associations with each other.

As our staff grew, our staff meetings became occasions for challenging each other to include voices however bizarre, but also occasions to question what sounded bizarre. It took a lot of courage, but I managed to overcome my hesitancy, my politeness, by asking Del, "You don't look like a woman to me. What makes you think you are a woman?" Del's appropriate answer: "What makes *you* think you are a woman?" The reply became a chance for more in-depth analysis and conversation.

We used the family metaphor a great deal in our church because it was the most suitable. As we became more comfortable with each other, we became more able to treat each other with the openness of family. We became, through our weekly worship together and eating together, much more like the family of the early church. The challenge was to widen the family to include both services working together.

In the morning service, the busyness of people's lives made church family intimacy more difficult. The more time a congregant spent in small-group activities or at church, the more they experienced this family ethos. We found that those who were evening service congregants tended to volunteer more consistently. During our high holidays, e.g., on Christmas Eve, where eating together became part of the experience, morning and evening congregants and strangers and newcomers shared table together. The queerer members taught by example, that the more involved one was, the more heightened the experience of an alternative community became. Morning congregants became more active as a result.

I noticed that newer families in the morning service that came from predominantly secular backgrounds also demanded more small-group participation. Again, the more morning service congregants lived and worked together as a "household," the more we became able to challenge, to question, to become a real community.

The queerness of this radical mix of people sharing one church home went largely unnoticed by all there, except for the Dels and Marys, who had experienced rejection everywhere else. But we began to experience, as comfort levels grew, how "queer" the most seemingly normal middle-class families really were. People felt more comfortable letting their queer sides show as they noticed those around them getting away with it.

This manifested itself in, for example, feeling free to swear in front of me, the minister, or crying in public, or admitting extramarital affairs, sexual dysfunction, same-sex experiences, and those life occurrences that in my experience aren't typically discussed in a church. This increased ease in intimacy brought about, in part, by the presence of the marginalized seemed to cut across age, race, and class divisions. I increasingly came to see the "facade" of normalcy break down the more our church family grew and grew comfortable crossing barriers.

It was as if, in the shadow of Derrida and the light of Christ, we could say that in allowing ourselves to give up any notions of "holiness," whatever that might mean, we were allowing ourselves honesty and community. In allowing ourselves to be "real," as one evening service person said, we allowed God to do the gifting. We couldn't and we didn't. By allowing church to be its sinful self, we all became a little freer to ask for what we needed from the household of God.

One of the first things we needed to confess was that we didn't have anything to offer anybody, other than food, prayer, the sharing of scripture, and shelter. Later, we were able to offer financial help, pastoral support, and community. Those like Del and Mary who were most marginalized came for the food and shelter, and tended to stay for everything else. We who were there before they came reminded ourselves and them over and over again that what we were sharing had always been there waiting for them. It was not ours to give. It was their inheritance.

The marginalized who came were so used to being the objects of charity or abuse or both that this message was reiterated every week and every day in one context or another. Some morning service people were often so used to seeing themselves as the givers of charity that the same message, that "they" are "us," was also necessary and necessarily repeated. No one would have listened if we hadn't also lived it out through our diversity and difference.

To deliver an inheritance, which was what the task of the church was to the queerest of queers, was the most difficult step. No one believed it. Over time more and more came to believe it, but only if it really meant what it said — if it meant food when you were hungry, money when you really needed money, love when you needed love, community all the time. Slowly, the evangelical message that the church (we) had to give to them was accepted. Even more slowly, they learned to assume the leadership and ownership that was theirs.

In return, the gift given to the church (before they arrived) was the church. We had forgotten, I believe, what church might look like, what church might have looked like in scriptural times. By forcing me and each other to reread scripture, the gift that queers brought was in line with the gift of the Holy Spirit. The gift was the call back or *religio* to faithfulness.

The church, before becoming consciously welcoming to difference and after, was caught up in the cycle of evangelism. The cycle of evangelism is, like gift giving, an impossible movement if not for the in-breaking of the Messiah.

And Back Again

To return to Blanchot's story that began this chapter and examine it more closely, let us imagine that the Messiah has come and is standing at the gates of the city among the poorest of the poor, a most biblical image. What is our response to the Messiah's presence? What should be our response to the Messiah's presence?

It is a parable, of course, that Blanchot has spun to demonstrate the necessity of keeping the question of ethicality, of justice, of right answers, forever open. The project of the nineteenth century, in a sense, was to answer all possible questions. The project of twentieth-century philosophy was, perhaps, to question all possible answers. The Christian, perhaps more than the secular person, would not want to ask anything of the Messiah at the gates of the city. But there is another response to her/his standing there. The response would be to fall down and worship, to feed and to clothe. Those actions we can perform.

We can become "them" and hope to be apostolic witnesses in the process. Not so much by the ruse of gift giving or answers but of simple hospitality, a biblical virtue that we discussed earlier. The hospitality would perhaps be giving the Messiah what is rightfully hers/his, the church and our lives. In this very childlike way, the church and queer theology answer the philosophical challenge. Yes, it is impossible for Christians or anyone else to be "good." It is impossible to give a true gift in this human life. What is possible is to give the possible Messiah his/her home back.

Conclusion

Queer Evangelism

Back Again, to the Beginning

I felt called in ordained ministry to grow my church. I began by thinking that evangelism meant adding people to the congregation. This quickly became complicated by another call, the call to care for the marginalized that surrounded our inner-city church, Emmanuel Howard Park United, on the border of Parkdale, one of the city's poorest neighborhoods. We began an evening service and dinner in direct reaction to an expressed need by poorer members of the community. Among the earliest participants were two transgendered individuals whom this study calls Del and Mary. Their participation and the participation of what I came to call a "continuum of queer" taught Emmanuel Howard Park an enormous amount about how to be a welcoming congregation. Their teaching us and prophesying to us and the move to reread scripture with queer eyes came to influence profoundly what any of us thought evangelism meant.

Our "learning to live with queerness" allowed us to "read" a Jesus who was queer (transgressive, odd, indecipherable). Thinking as queer (differently, welcoming the strangeness of our faith and scripture, learning to love the gaps and contradictions, feeling comfort in the movement rather than the answer) allowed us to become queer theologians. Becoming queer theologians allowed us to welcome others as queer (always and never the originators, never and always the recipients) evangelists.

To capture a "snapshot" of the process that seemed to be underway at Emmanuel Howard Park, and one that might assist other clergy and laity who had struggled to "grow" their churches in an inclusive environment (one welcoming lesbigay and trans as full members), I structured a research study around the question, How do the transgendered (possibly the queerest of the queer) in our society challenge the theory and practice of evangelism?

I began with an attempt to investigate the term "queer," not so much as to constrain it but to allow it to be the fluid center of what increasingly came to be seen as the movement of evangelism. Judith Butler was among those theorists used for that purpose. Jacques Derrida and other thinkers often referred to as "postmodernist" or "poststructuralist" were involved because of their qu(e)erying of philosophy. Derrida's work on the impossibility of gift giving was particularly appropriate since evangelism was often seen as the church gifting the secular world.

I tried to allow the theorists to converse with the theologians as well as have both speak to our experience with Del and Mary and others. Along with contemporary voices and examples in the church growth movement as well as mentors in other churches, I attempted to bring in the scriptural voices of the New Testament as the queerly (not really) original conversation. I hoped to allow Jesus Christ, the object and subject of the conversation, to continue as *the* question. The conversation itself came to seem part of the evangelical flux.

The purpose of the theoretical study was and is to allow the questions scripture raises to be seen as enough in themselves. One of the purposes of the research study came to be to allow the voices that might otherwise not be heard, to be heard (otherwise).

To that end, we conducted six case studies, allowing the participants to become active meaning makers in the design of the project. Case studies were chosen, as the cases (certainly of Del and Mary) were relatively unique. This was done as qualitative rather than quantitative research, its results used to provide another conversational partner with the theorists and scriptures involved. I hoped to provide, as Creswell indicates, an "oral history" of the changes occurring at Emmanuel Howard Park and in our own thinking.[1] Purposeful sampling of the interviews and of other conversations with congregants at EHP over the years were combined, resulting in what I hoped

---

1. J. Creswell, *Qualitative Inquiry and Research Design: Choosing among Five Traditions* (Thousand Oaks, Calif.: Sage Publications, 1998).

would be holistic analysis of the material gleaned. Phenomenologically, this study also included my experience and my bias as part of the story. Themes emerged, I hoped, where answers did not. A few themes coalesced along with those indicated above.

Scripture is a "queer" read. It is unlike any other book in that God inspires human witnesses to record God's actions, and yet it is the word of proximate witnesses and not the word of God untranslated. It is an earthen vessel, yet to paraphrase Luther, one that contains Christ. The text that has been interpreted, exegeted, and reinvented, the text that comes to us as wounded by its interventions as the body of Christ on the cross is wounded, is also read by us through faculties dimmed by our world. It tells us the truth, but we might never read the "truth" out of it. Our sin, our humanness intervenes throughout the process. Its sin, its humanness meets us on every page.

We are queer beings existing on a continuum of queer. The more we understand each other intimately, the more queer (different, unusual, abnormal) we seem to be. **A church that allows us to be as queer as we feel, feels welcoming to queers (those that exist on the margins). This is a high-demand church in the areas of Christian formation, because difference is difficult. This is a church that cannot ever claim to "know" either scripture or Christ in the immediate sense and cannot claim to pass along anything but proximate witness to anyone. Church must humble itself to welcome the queerest of the queer.**

When we are called by Christ, through scripture, to "preach the good news," we are in a sense defeated before we begin because we do not understand what it is we are saying or why we are saying it. Knowing this, however, only means that we should "preach the good news" with more fervor and more confidence. For what we have been given by the power of the Holy Spirit is Christ's presence when we preach, and Christ will be present to the other to whom we preach. This is Christ's promise, not ours. We are forever humbled by the encounter with Christ and them, our neighbors. We, in the words of deconstruction, are commanded to give economy, the economy of the "gift," its chance.

Scripture also informs us that the knock at the door of the temple is critical. The Word is not in the purview of the temple, or of our

church, but comes to us from the outside, for God is active in the world. The conversation is between the world and the church. The conversion is of the church as well as of the world. Whether Christ is at the temple doors or Paul is writing to the early churches, we are called back from the outside to faithfulness. Prophets of our own God as well as prophets of other gods exist outside, and we are called to discern between them. One scriptural test is that if they ask to be baptized, if they ask to be let in, they should be let in.

Hospitality, the ethical imperative that runs through scripture, must be the imperative that runs through church life. This also is invitational to the outside. And once inside, it radically affects the way to do church. Hospitality extends throughout the week and prevents "us" and "them" thinking. If anything, the biblical witness says that the marginalized are the necessary inheritors of the church and its rightful owners. If this is not reflected in our structures or our pews, if we are not allowed to be our queer selves, our church is in danger of being more club than church. Hospitality precludes "moralizing" as a function of church, precludes judging.

The biblical witness, however, always cautions that we will err, we will fail, we will not create heaven on earth even as we are charged by the same scripture to look toward nothing less.

The biblical witness also states that God will not fail, that Christ will return, so that, in Christ, our triumph is guaranteed.

Evangelism Rethought

The evening service proved to be an act of evangelism. The initiator of the evangelism was and is the Holy Spirit. We, as church before the evening service, out of a renewed sense of the scriptural call to be inclusive, opened our doors with a specific imperative to welcome the marginalized. Our message was the good and inclusively good news of the gospel. We began with no particular expectation as to what might happen next. What happened next was an evangelism of our church. We were pushed to continue welcoming. Would we really prove to be a church of the New Testament? Could we live with inclusion liturgically, theologically, communally?

The evangelists were the marginalized, the secular, and ourselves. Our "work" was to "get out of the way" of the Spirit. This we discovered was a "queer" process. It was based on a queer reading of scripture, a queer living-out of family and community, and resulted in queers being comfortable in our church. It also resulted in a queer (unusual, transgressive, sexually marginalized, different) church. One of the results is that we began to see ourselves as Christian and therefore queer (marginalized, fringe, different).

The research question that had inspired this project was, "How do the transgendered (possibly the queerest of the queer) in our society challenge the theory and practice of evangelism?" The answer we both lived and discovered was that evangelism ceased to be an action of ours at all. Evangelism is experienced as an action upon the church, as response to that action and is based in a queer scripture read queerly. Evangelism is experienced as hospitality to the marginalized and hospitality from the marginalized commencing in the life, death, and resurrection of Jesus Christ. Evangelism is the work of the Holy Spirit in which we, as Christians and as messengers to Christians and others, get caught up. The most likely vehicles of evangelism will be, in any situation, the queerest of the queer.

Evangelism is both praxis and theory/theology. Evangelism is the preaching of the good news of Jesus Christ in action and word from the inside out and the outside in. Evangelism is gift given by God and testified to by a church which was both inside and outside the doors of our church. What we embarked upon was a journey into humility, into queerness in all its guises, into difference — where difference became not something to be hidden but the mark of the repentant and forgiven Christian.

This study, of course, is an event of a living, breathing community that exists in a real inner city, just as Del and Mary are living, breathing individuals who live in a real inner city. The experiment and experience is growing, evolving, and changing, and we have no idea of its long-range possibilities or probabilities. This is only a snapshot of a new/old, hopefully faithful community of Christians who are both sinners and saints. The ramifications, however, we hope, are immense. We hope — we including Del and Mary — that other inner-city churches come to understand themselves as queer. We certainly pray that they see themselves as household to the marginalized, as hospitable to everyone. If they do, after living this project we believe chances are that they will discover themselves as queer. They will also discover themselves as qu(e)erying many of their culturally conditioned assumptions about what Christianity is and was. The movement of evangelism as evidenced scripturally was a movement of Christ calling, upholding, and sending forth. Even if we (wrongly I have tried to argue) equate Christ unilaterally with church, it is still a movement of call first, then healing/sustaining, then sending out.

The theology of call always sees the initiative with Christ to us. "Us," we have come to interpret, means us. That is, the call of Christ does not end with our becoming Christian, joining a church, becoming ordinands, or any of the above, but is a continuous and ever-changing invitation. Yet we so often seem to see "call" as a onetime story or a conversion "experience." In like manner, the evangelical movement seems to be interpreted as ending in baptism or joining a church or some moment rather than as a continuous movement in which we become caught up.

The continuity of the calling, upholding, and sending is ever initiated by Christ, never by us. We become part of the story, part of scripture if you will, part of the community of faith. **The movement of evangelism *is* the life of the Christian.** It is not a deed done by a Christian. To look at evangelism is to examine this cycle, similar to the economy of the gift in Derrida or the call of the other in Levinas. For the queer evangelist the fact that evangelism is the Christian life is critical, for the call always breaks into the cycle from the outside. If you will, the movement is from the margin to the center, to the margin again.

Epilogue

Again, Beginning

Dear Reader,

As this book evolved, so does the day-to-day life of the living organism called Emmanuel Howard Park United Church. I feel the need to leave the reader (and the read) with the most up-to-date snapshot possible before publication. It is also necessary to acknowledge, yet again, that which the Holy Spirit has wrought in our midst.

The church continues to grow as if to embarrass us. For the first time in twenty or so years it is close to breaking even financially and no longer needs to use a trust fund bequeathed to it, a trust fund that is now depleted. If you were to attend on an average Sunday morning you would witness around 120 adults at worship and 40 to 60 children in Sunday school. Our evening service sees around 30 to 40 at worship and 70 to 80 at the community dinner that is now sustained by food agencies in our community. This is still not enough to fill the sanctuary that could hold 500 or so, but on Christmas Eve we have come close.

We operate with a paid staff of one full-time clergy person (myself), one very part-time spiritual director who facilitates retreats and provides individual direction, a large community of musicians who perform now and then and some soloists who perform frequently, three part-time Sunday school teachers, a part-time caretaker, and a part-time secretary. Added to this are a core of about fifteen to twenty highly committed and involved volunteers who give a great deal of their time to church activity. The rental of the building to groups whose mission statements are compatible with ours — for example, a healing center, community kitchen, twelve-step groups — pays for the maintenance of the building.

There is a plethora of small groups and Bible study opportunities, and our experience is that the more marginalized and queer people are, the more active they become in these small groups. Our groups continue to be completely integrated along "choice" rather than biological lines. That means that some lesbians attend men's groups and trans folk attend women's groups (at the time of this writing we have no female-to-male trans members). We have added to our seniors' services in that we now have, besides our lunches and card games, a seniors' appreciation Sunday where all receive an invitation to attend.

Trying to create a safe place for crack addicts, street people, as well as children has presented demands that we've met by providing volunteer security and starting our afternoon drop-in well after the morning service Sunday school classes have vacated. Being inclusive must mean being inclusive of children, and we ask our drop-in folk to come back later if they wander in before the afternoon, although everyone is always welcome at worship whether morning or night.

Over the years, we've had to ask certain people to leave with the understanding that the door is forever open if their behavior changes. Behavior that we've found unacceptable is any behavior that prevents others from being able to feel welcomed. Threats, obscene or abusive language, overt racism, and threatening homophobia don't belong in a true sanctuary, although we have always tried to mitigate, peace keep, rather than ban.

At times, we've had to ask those to leave whose mental illness threatened to dominate and distract to such a degree that others felt unsafe. These occasions are always awful and painful and seem to us to be admissions of failure, which they are. We are human and we are not God, and therefore our inclusion has its limits. Inherent in such moments is the fine line between the reality that an important teaching and messenger might be lost because of concerns for the safety of other congregants. We painfully admit that this is possible and so try to include wherever we can.

Of course, congregants still leave of their own volition, to decamp to other cities or countries, because of misunderstandings with other congregants and changes in their own families (divorce, for example). Few these days leave because of the increased queerness of the place. The ones who inhabit the pews know and have made a conscious choice by now to be part of a queer church.

We still exhibit as humans all those charming little traits like jealousy, vanity, paranoia, and sheer exhaustion. We still exhibit as Christians those holy virtues such as compassion, forgiveness, and, that most saving of graces, a sense of humor about all our human foibles.

We are, in short, still a real family, a real queer family. We have grown in struggle and joy, and those who have hung in since the beginning of our journey, and the many who have been there even before I came, are truly saints. We ultimately are a community in waiting for the one who will, we are promised, arrive at some point: Christ.

We are part of a mainline denomination and have been supported by their funds at various times of our existence. A grant from the Mission and Service fund helped bridge the gap between almost breaking even and breaking even. A grant from a Toronto United Church Council funding group paid for an advertising campaign that our members designed with slogans like, "I go because I am loved there," "I go because I am challenged there," with the statement, "Come and find out why you belong." Our own congregants' faces graced these bus shelter and streetcar and subway ads. All queer in varying degrees.

The ads generated a flurry of media interest. I reiterated over and over again that this was not a marketing move, and it was not intended to "grow" the church, but rather was intended to welcome those who felt unwelcomed in other places of worship. Sometimes the reporters heard and sometimes they didn't. The articles themselves became part of the movement of evangelism in that they described our queerness and therefore other queers came. I start every service now with a welcome-home message. "This is not my church. It is not our church. It is not the United Church of Canada's church. It is your church. It was bequeathed to you by your ancestors in the faith. Welcome to your home."

When my license was threatened by the government for marrying two women before the law had changed, the broader church was mute and I was bailed out by our national television network and a civil rights lawyer. Though the government backed down, and then, of course, we all rejoiced when the law was overturned, I remember the moment. When I announced the celebration we had over the legalizing of same-sex marriage, our local presbytery greeted the news in a stony silence. We are an affirming denomination, but then again are we? Institutions, even the best of ones, are institutions. Our church remains supported by and supportive of the broader church, but we know that in most ways that matter we are on our own.

You may ask as you conclude this portion of the journey with us — what about me, Rev. Dr. Cheri DiNovo? Where do I find myself now? After all, I've been at the center of this journey in a sense and am still standing.

The deaths have hurt the most. As I write this, Mary is dead. Mary died in a prison close to the home of her birth on the prairies. The prison authorities had transferred her there to serve her five-year sentence. She had written me long, beautiful, moving letters about how in prison she had sobered up, how she had reconnected with her biological family who still lived on a reserve. Her sister had become an addiction counselor, and Mary was so proud of her. She was living life in prison as a female even though she was incarcerated in an all-male facility. Her photo displayed a beautiful female face, fully made up, above a male prison uniform. Yes, she had been raped continuously, but she had a new lover. He had painted a portrait of her. I immediately hung it on my office wall, where it still remains. "I miss you all. You were my real family." Her local pimp and lover came to the evening service and dinner. He wept. We turned the evening service into a funeral service for her. Another transgendered woman, Mary's sponsor, came and stayed, becoming a member of the church.

There were other deaths of those who, queer as they were, simply could not survive the world. One of them, a young bisexual Asian woman addicted to prescription drugs, died from an overdose. She had become a trusted and constant church volunteer. She was one of those who called me many times daily in various states of inebriation, and I had learned to ignore her calls unless they sounded desperate. They almost always sounded desperate. It was just a matter of time, but somehow I had always managed to intuit when the situation was serious enough to intervene. I miscalculated. She died, and the whole church turned out to mourn. Other older and more stable members died, and their deaths, though natural, left marks. Their photographs adorn our walls. They have become part of the DNA of the place.

And then, yes, the inevitable happened. Del died. I knew she had gone back to chipping at morphine. Somehow, perhaps because she had survived so much and done it so independently, I and others missed all the warning signs. Del was the most dependable person, and I knew that when she missed a rehearsal there was a serious problem. I called and followed up. So did many. After all, we thought, she was in the best of spirits. She had been practicing for a Caribbean service with other local musicians and was looking forward to an exciting event, one with the Riverside, New York, church step-dancing team as special guests. She was surrounded now by a community and a family that loved her and needed her. She had formed us. She had taught us. We were hers. And she was ours. So when Del said that, just like the crack incident, she could handle her own withdrawal, I believed her.

I had lunch with her days before. Friends, other musicians, had seen her the night before. She was not depressed. She was as strong as we had ever seen her. No one will ever know what actually happened. No one ever knows what actually happens. She was found in her bathtub. We know she was weaning herself off morphine. We know she was not suicidal. We know nothing else. We will never know anything else. What is it that we ever know?

When Del died we discovered all those facts about her life she had so carefully shielded from us. She had been one of North America's foremost studio keyboard musicians. She had performed (under her male name, of course) with many of the greats of the century in jazz and country and blues. We saw pictures of her as a he. I spoke to her biological family for the first time, even though Del was more a part of our family. Her past opened up in ways she never would have wished (or would she?). We were engulfed with the world and suffering and yet her funeral, that ironically filled the church, was an outpouring of the grief of the Christian.

"Del was the most exclusive of performers. She only played for the poor," I eulogized. She could have played anywhere, but she played for us. Under her typical jeans and T-shirt, friends dressed her in a miniskirt, found in her room. The softness of femininity plumped her cheeks (or was it embalming fluid?). The ironic smile remained.

As I write this, dear reader, I pour myself the second glass of wine and still am barely able to recall how awesome is the moment, how holy is the awareness, that is graced by the trace of the *tout autre*. There is not a minute of any day that we as a community consciously or unconsciously do not remember her impact. This is what it felt like to be one of the disciples and remember. We are the disciples, and we do remember. There was a Christ. This much we know.

So, dear friends, in the manner of our faith's epistles, I would have to say that I have survived humbled. I will never be the same. It is not easy to invite difference into your life and the life of your church. It is not joyful or liberative or rewarding or enriching. It brings suffering. It also brings the closest experience to heaven that we will ever have in this life.

I picture the women huddled around the cross and then waiting outside the empty tomb. Was the cross not horror? Was the road to Emmaus not ecstasy? I can be sure of only one reality in this church, and that is death. I can guarantee only one experience, and that is bliss.

I know less now than when I started. It is absolutely clear to me that tomorrow this church could either close or expand. It is definite that our queer family will either die or live. Outside of these sure aspects, God only knows. As long as our doors are open, though, the queer evangelist will arrive. We pray she/he will. Our prayers have already been answered.

In Christ,
Cheri

Bibliography

Abraham, William J. *The Logic of Evangelism*. Grand Rapids, Mich.: Eerd-mans, 1989.

Archer, Bert. *The End of Gay and the Death of Heterosexuality*. Toronto: Doubleday, 1999.

Bandy, Tom. *Kicking Habits*. Toronto: United Church Publishing, 1997.

Barnett, Victoria. *For the Soul of the People*. New York: Oxford, 1992.

Barth, Karl. *Church Dogmatics*. Vol. 1.1. Edinburgh: T. & T. Clark, 1975.

———. *Church Dogmatics: A Selection*. Grand Rapids, Mich.: Eerdmans, 1991.

———. *The Faith of the Church*. New York: Meridian, 1958.

———. *The Gottingen Dogmatics*. Grand Rapids, Mich.: Eerdmans, 1991.

———. *The Theology of John Calvin*. Grand Rapids, Mich.: Eerdmans, 1995.

Berg, Bruce. *Qualitative Research Methods for the Social Sciences*. Boston: Allyn and Bacon, 1998.

Bibby, Reginald. *Fragmented Gods: The Poverty and Potential of Religion in Canada*. Toronto: Irwin, 1997.

———. *There's Got to Be More*. Winfield, B.C.: Wood Lake Books, 1995.

———. *Unknown Gods: The Ongoing Story of Religion in Canada* (Toronto: Stoddart, 1993

Bonhoeffer, Dietrich. *The Cost of Discipleship*. New York: Simon & Schuster, 1959.

———. *Life Together*. New York: Harper, 1954.

———. *The Martyred Christian*. New York: Collier Books, 1983.

Borges, Jorge Luis. *Ficciones*. New York: Grove Press, 1962.

Brown, Joanna, and Carole Bohn, eds. *Christianity, Patriarchy and Abuse*. New York: Pilgrim Press, 1989.

Brown, Raymond E. *The Churches the Apostles Left Behind*. New York: Paulist Press, 1984.

Butler, Judith. *Bodies That Matter: On the Discursive Limits of "Sex."* New York: Routledge, 1993.

———. *Gender Trouble*. New York: Routledge, 1999.

Callahan, Ken. *12 Steps to an Effective Church*. New York: HarperCollins, 1987.

Calvin, John. *Institutes of the Christian Religion*. Edited by John T. McNeill. Philadelphia: Westminster Press, 1969.

Caputo, John. *Deconstruction in a Nutshell*. New York: Fordham, 1997.

————. *The Prayers and Tears of Jacques Derrida*. Bloomington: Indiana University Press, 1997.

————. *Radical Hermeneutics*. Bloomington: Indiana University Press, 1987.

Clapp, Rodney. *Families at the Crossroads*. Downers Grove, Ill.: InterVarsity Press, 1993.

Creswell, John W. *Qualitative Inquiry and Research Design: Choosing among Five Traditions*. Thousand Oaks, Calif.: Sage Publications, 1998.

Daly, Mary. *Gyn/Ecology*. Boston: Beacon Press, 1990.

Deleuze, Gilles, and Felix Guattari. *A Thousand Plateaus*. Minneapolis: University of Minnesota Press, 1987.

Demson, David. *Hans Frei and Karl Barth*. Grand Rapids, Mich.: Eerdmans, 1997.

Derrida, Jacques. *Derrida and Negative Theology*. Edited by Harold Coward and Toby Foshay. Albany: State University of New York, 1992.

————. *The Gift of Death*. Chicago: University of Chicago Press, 1995.

————. *Given Time. 1, Counterfeit Money* Chicago: University of Chicago Press, 1992.

————. *Languages of the Unsayable: The Play of Negativity in Literature and Literary Theory*. New York: Columbia University Press, 1989.

————. *Passions*. Paris: Galilee, 1993.

Derrida, Jacques, and Gianni Vattimo. *Religion*. Stanford, Calif.: Stanford University Press, 1996.

Dinoia, J. A. *The Diversity of Religions*. Washington, D.C.: Catholic University of America Press, 1992.

Easum, William. *How to Reach Baby Boomers*. Nashville: Abingdon Press, 1991.

Foucault, Michel. *The Order of Things: An Archaeology of the Human Sciences*. New York: Pantheon, 1971.

————. *The History of Sexuality*. Vol. 1. New York: Pantheon, 1978.

————. *The History of Sexuality*. Vol. 2. *An Introduction*. Translated by R. Hurley. New York: Pantheon, 1978.

————. *Discipline and Punish*. New York: Random House, 1979.

————. "What Is Enlightenment?" In *The Foucault Reader*, edited by Paul Rabinow. New York: Pantheon Books, 1984.

————. *Remarks on Marx: Conversations with Ducio Trombadori*. Translated by R. James Goldstein and James Cascaito. New York: Semiotext(e), 1991.

Fulkerson, Mary McClintock. "Gender — Being It or Doing It? The Church, Homosexuality and the Politics of Identity." In *Que(e)rying Religion: A Critical Anthology*, ed. David Comstock and Susan E. Henking. New York: Continuum, 1997.

Gallagher, Michael. *Clashing Symbols*. Mahwah, N.J.: Paulist Press, 1984.

Gerrish, Brian. *Grace and Reason: A Study in the Theology of Luther.* Oxford: Oxford University Press, 1962.

Gross, Sally. *Intersexuality and Scripture. www.bfpubs.demon.co.uk/sally.htm.*

Guinness, Oz. *Dining with the Devil.* Grand Rapids, Mich.: Baker Book House, 1993.

Hall, Douglas John. *The Future of the Church.* Toronto: United Church Publishing, 1989.

Halperin, David. *One Hundred Years of Homosexuality.* New York: Routledge, 1990.

————. *Saint Foucault: Towards a Gay Hagiography.* New York: Oxford, 1995.

Hanchey, Howard. *Church Growth and the Power of Evangelism.* Cambridge, Mass.: Cowley Publications, 1990.

Hoge, Dean, Benton Johnson, and Donald Luidens. *Vanishing Boundaries.* Louisville: Westminster John Knox, 1994.

Hunter, George G., III. *How to Reach Secular People.* Nashville: Abingdon, 1992.

Hybels, Bill. *Becoming a Contagious Christian.* Grand Rapids, Mich.: Zondervan, 1994.

————. *Evangelism.* Grand Rapids, Mich.: Zondervan, 1996.

Irigaray, Luce. *The Ethics of Sexual Difference.* New York: Cornell, 1993.

Kaplan, Abraham. *The Conduct of Inquiry.* Scranton, Pa.: Chandler Publishing, 1998.

Kearney, Richard. *The Continental Philosophy Reader.* New York: Routledge, 1996.

Keller, Catherine. *Apocalypse Now and Then: A Feminist Guide to the End of the World.* Boston: Beacon, 1996.

Killen, Patricia O'Connell, and John deBeer. *The Art of Theological Reflection.* New York: Crossroad, 1994.

Kinast, Robert. *Let Ministry Teach.* Collegeville, Minn.: Liturgical Press, 1996.

Kirby, Sandra, and Kate McKenna. *Experience, Research, Social Change: Methods from the Margins.* Toronto: Garamond Press, 1989.

Kristeva, Julia. *Nations without Nationalism.* New York: Columbia University Press, 1993.

Lawrence, Bruce B. *Defenders of God.* San Francisco: Harper & Row, 1989.

Levan, Christopher. *God Hates Religion.* Toronto: United Church Publishing, 1995.

Levinas, Emmanuel. *Otherwise Than Being, or Beyond Essence.* Translated by Alphonso Lingis. Dordrecht: Martinus Nijhoff, 1981.

Lindbeck, George. *The Nature of Doctrine: Religion and Theology in a Postliberal Age.* Louisville: Westminster John Knox, 1984.

Lyotard, Jean-François. *The Postmodern Condition: A Report on Knowledge, Theory and Literature.* Minneapolis: University of Minnesota Press, 1984.

Machaffie, Barbara. *Her Story.* Philadelphia: Fortress Press, 1986.

Messer, Donald. *Contemporary Images of Christian Ministry*. Nashville: Abingdon Press, 1989.

Middleton, Richard J. & Brian J. Walsh. *Truth Is Stranger Than It Used to Be*. Downers Grove, Ill.: InterVarsity Press, 1995.

Milbank, John, Catherine Pickstock, and Graham Ward, eds. *Radical Orthodoxy*. London: Routledge, 1999.

Moi, Toril. *Sexual/Textual Politics*. New York: Routledge, 1996.

Moltmann, Jürgen. *The Church in the Power of the Spirit*. London: SCM Press, 1977.

Moore, Stephen. *God's Gym*. New York: Routledge, 1996.

————, ed. *The Postmodern Bible*. New Haven, Conn.: Yale University Press, 1995.

Myers, William. *Research in Ministry: A Primer for the Doctor of Ministry Program*. Chicago: Exploration Press, 1997.

Neill, Stephen. *A History of Christian Missions*. London: Penguin, 1984.

Paris, Peter J., et al. *The History of the Riverside Church in the City of New York*. New York: New York University Press, 2004.

Pippin, Tina. *Death and Desire*. Louisville: Westminster John Knox, 1992.

Posterski, Don, and Irwin Barker. *Where's a Good Church?* Winfield, B.C.: Wood Lake Books, 1993.

Posterski, Don, and Gary Nelson. *Future Faith Churches*. Winfield, B.C.: Wood Lake Books, 1997.

Pritchard, G. A. *Willow Creek Seeker Services*. Grand Rapids, Mich.: Baker Books, 1994.

Rabinow, Paul, ed. *The Foucault Reader*. New York: Pantheon Books, 1984.

Ricoeur, Paul. *Freud and Philosophy: An Essay on Interpretation*. New Haven, Conn.: Yale University Press, 1970.

Rogers, Eugene F., Jr. *Sexuality and the Christian Body*. Oxford: Blackwell, 1999.

Roof, Wade, & William McKinney. *American Mainline Religion: Its Changing Shape and Future*. New Brunswick, N.J.: Rutgers University Press, 1987.

Rudy, Kathy. *Sex and the Church*. Boston: Beacon, 1997.

Ruether, Rosemary Radford. *Sexism and Godtalk: Toward a Feminist Theology*. Boston: Beacon, 1983.

Russell, Keith A. *In Search of the Church*. New York: Alban Institute, 1994.

Russell, Letty M. *Church in the Round: Feminist Interpretation of the Church*. Louisville: Westminster John Knox, 1993.

Sample, Tex. *Hard Living People and Mainstream Christianity*. Nashville: Abingdon, 1993.

Schaller, Lyle. *Growing Plans*. Nashville: Abingdon, 1983.

————. *Innovations in Ministry: Models for the 21st Century*. Nashville: Abingdon, 1994.

Schleiermacher, Friedrich. *On Religion.* New York: Cambridge University Press, 1998.

Schmalenberger, Jerry. *Called to Witness.* Lima: C.S.S. Publishing, 1993.

Schneider, Laurel C. "Homosexuality, Queer Theory, and Christian Theology." *Religious Studies Review* 26 (2000): 3.

Schüssler-Fiorenza, Elisabeth. *Bread Not Stone.* Boston: Beacon Press, 1989.

———. *In Memory of Her.* New York: Crossroad, 1984.

Schwartz, Christian, and Christoph Schalk. *Implementation Guide to Natural Church Development.* Carol Stream, Ill.: ChurchSmart Resources, 1998.

Sinclair, Donna, and Christopher White. *Jacob's Blessing.* Kelowna, B.C.: Wood Lake Books, 1999.

Smith, Donald. *How to Attract and Keep Church Members.* Louisville: Westminster John Knox, 1992.

Spong, John Shelby. *Living in Sin: A Bishop Rethinks Sexuality.* San Francisco: HarperSanFrancisco, 1990.

Stein, Gertrude. *Portraits and Prayers.* Boston: Beacon Press, 1957.

Steinberg, Leo. *The Sexuality of Christ in Renaissance Art and in Modern Oblivion.* Chicago: University of Chicago Press, 1996.

Student Christian Movement. "Homophobia in the Churches." Toronto: photocopied, 1999.

Tanis, Justin. *Transgendered: Theology, Ministry, and Communities of Faith.* Cleveland: Pilgrim Press, 2003.

Tanner, Kathryn. *Theories of Culture: A New Agenda for Theology.* Minneapolis: Augsburg, 1997.

Taylor, Mark C. *Erring: A Postmodern A/Theology.* Chicago: University of Chicago Press, 1987.

———. *Nots.* Chicago: University of Chicago, 1993.

Thatcher, Adran, and Elizabeth Stuart, eds. *Sexuality and Gender.* Grand Rapids, Mich.: Eerdmans, 1996.

Thiemann, Ronald, and William Placher, eds. *Why Are We Here?* Harrisburg, Pa.: Trinity Press, 1989.

Ward, Graham. *Barth, Derrida and the Language of Theology.* Cambridge: Cambridge University Press, 1995.

———, ed. *The Postmodern God.* Oxford: Blackwell, 1997.

Whitehead, Evelyn and James. *Method in Ministry.* Kansas City, Mo.: Sheed & Ward, 1995.